# Gender in Early Mode

This concise and stimulating book explores the history of gender in England between 1500 and 1700. The second edition has been thoroughly revised to include new material on global connections, masculinity and recent historiography.

Amid the upheavals of the Reformation and Civil Wars, gender was political. Sexual difference and women's roles were matters of public debate, while social and economic changes were impacting on work, family and marriage. The rich archives of law, state and family testify to the complex configurations of patriarchal order and resistance to it. *Gender in Early Modern England* provides insight into gender relations in a time when a stark hierarchy of gender co-existed with a surprising degree of female capacity, great potential for challenge and confrontation, and a persistent sense of the mystery of the body. Documents include early feminist argument, law, midwives' books, recipes, protest, sexual insults, cross-dressers, women escaping slavery, royal favourites and petitions.

With a chronology, who's who, glossary, guide to further reading and previously unpublished archival documents, *Gender in Early Modern England* is the perfect resource for all students interested in the history of women and gender in England between 1500 and 1700.

**Laura Gowing** is Professor of Early Modern History at King's College, London and the author of several books and articles on the history of women, sexuality and the body. Her most recent publication is *Ingenious Trade: Women and Work in Seventeenth-Century London* (2021).

# Seminar Studies

History is the narrative constructed by historians from traces left by the past. Historical enquiry is often driven by contemporary issues and, in consequence, historical narratives are constantly reconsidered, reconstructed and reshaped. The fact that different historians have different perspectives on issues means that there is often controversy and no universally agreed version of past events. *Seminar Studies* was designed to bridge the gap between current research and debate, and the broad, popular general surveys that often date rapidly.

The volumes in the series are written by historians who are not only familiar with the latest research and current debates concerning their topic, but who have themselves contributed to our understanding of the subject. The books are intended to provide the reader with a clear introduction to a major topic in history. They provide both a narrative of events and a critical analysis of contemporary interpretations. They include the kinds of tools generally omitted from specialist monographs: a chronology of events, a glossary of terms and brief biographies of 'who's who'. They also include bibliographical essays in order to guide students to the literature on various aspects of the subject. Students and teachers alike will find that the selection of documents will stimulate the discussion and offer insight into the raw materials used by historians in their attempt to understand the past.

Clive Emsley and Gordon Martel
Series Editors

# Gender in Early Modern England

Second Edition

Laura Gowing

Routledge
Taylor & Francis Group

LONDON AND NEW YORK

Cover image: Jan Steen, *Celebrating the Birth*, 1664. © Artefact/Alamy Stock Photo. In this Dutch genre painting a newly delivered mother is shown with her female family, friends, servants and her husband, holding the baby; behind, a young man mocks the father by making a cuckold sign with his fingers. The warming pan in the foreground echoes a contemporary saying that the only warmth in the marriage bed is the warming-pan, and the broken eggs could symbolise the loss of virginity.

Second edition published
by Routledge
4 Park Square, Milton Park, Abingdon, Oxon OX14 4RN

and by Routledge
605 Third Avenue, New York, NY 10158

*Routledge is an imprint of the Taylor & Francis Group, an informa business*

© 2023 Laura Gowing

[First edition published by Pearson Education Limited 2012]

*British Library Cataloguing in Publication Data*
A catalogue record for this book is available from the British Library

*Library of Congress Cataloging-in-Publication Data*
Names: Gowing, Laura, author.
Title: Gender in early modern england / Laura Gowing.
Description: Second edition. | Abingdon, Oxon ; New York, NY : Routledge, 2023. |
Series: Seminar studies | First edition published under title: Gender relations in early modern England. | Includes bibliographical references and index.
Identifiers: LCCN 2022016424 (print) | LCCN 2022016425 (ebook) | ISBN 9780367548322 (hbk) | ISBN 9780367548292 (pbk) | ISBN 9781003090786 (ebk)
Subjects: LCSH: Women--England--Social conditions--16th century. | Women--England--Social conditions--17th century. | Sex role--England--History--16th century. | Sex role--England--History--17th century.
Classification: LCC HQ1149.G7 G69 2023 (print) | LCC HQ1149.G7 (ebook) | DDC 305.4094209/031--dc23
LC record available at https://lccn.loc.gov/2022016424
LC ebook record available at https://lccn.loc.gov/2022016425

ISBN: 978-0-367-54832-2 (hbk)
ISBN: 978-0-367-54829-2 (pbk)
ISBN: 978-1-003-09078-6 (ebk)

DOI: 10.4324/9781003090786

Typeset in Sabon
by Taylor & Francis Books

# Contents

# Figures

# Chronology

| | |
|---|---|
| **1642** | Civil War breaks out; disestablishment of Church of England and abolition of church courts |
| **1642–6** | First Civil War |
| **1648–9** | Second Civil War; execution of Charles I |
| **1650** | Adultery made capital offence (repealed 1660) |
| **1651** | Parliamentary Victory |
| **1653** | Commonwealth: Oliver Cromwell Lord Protector, married to Elizabeth Cromwell |
| **1658** | Death of Oliver Cromwell |
| **1660** | Restoration of Charles II, married to Catherine of Braganza |
| **1679–81** | Exclusion Crisis |
| **1685** | Accession of James II, married to (1) Anne Hyde and (2) Mary of Modena |
| **1688** | Warming Pan Scandal |
| **1688** | Glorious Revolution |
| **1689** | Coronation of William III and Mary II |
| **1694** | Death of Mary II; William ruled alone |
| **1702** | Accession of Anne |

# Who's Who

**Mary Astell (1666–1731)**  Writer of feminist and other tracts, Anglican and Tory, single, educated at home, daughter of a Newcastle coal merchant.

**Elizabeth Barton (*c*.1506–34)**  Called the 'Nun of Kent'; Benedictine nun and visionary, previously a farm servant; prophesied that Henry VIII's proposed divorce from Katherine of Aragon would be the end of his reign; eventually executed.

**Margaret Cavendish (1623–73)**  Aristocrat writer and scientist; royalist; married William Cavendish; wrote poetry, natural philosophy, science fiction and memoir.

**Elizabeth Cellier (fl. 1668–88)**  Known as the Popish Midwife, she was implicated in 1679 in the 'Meal Tub Plot' against the future James II and acquitted on trial for treason. Her published self-defence led to another trial and the pillory. She later published a plan for a corporation of midwives.

**Sarah Churchill, née Jenyns, Duchess of Marlborough (1660–1744)**  Lady of the Bedchamber to Queen Anne; married Edward Churchill; Whig.

**Lady Anne Clifford (1590–1676)**  Baroness, diarist, involved in extensive lawsuit over her inheritance; educated by tutor; married Richard Sackville and Edward Herbert.

**Sir Edward Coke (1552–1634)**  Lord Chief Justice under James I; jurist, MP, defender of the common law; married Bridget Paston.

**Moll Cutpurse (Mary Frith) (1584–1659)**  Infamous thief, the subject of plays and stories.

**Galen of Pergamon (129–*c*.216)**  Greek physician in the Roman Empire, practitioner of anatomy and scholar of Hippocratic theory.

**Matthew Hopkins (*c*.1620–47)**  Self-appointed witchfinder based in East Anglia in the 1640s.

**Abigail Masham, née Hill, Baroness Masham (1670–1734)**   Cousin to Sarah Churchill, and favourite of Queen Anne, in whose household she became 'Mother of the Maids'; Tory; married Samuel Masham.

**Samuel Pepys (1633–1703)**   Diarist, naval administrator and MP; married Elizabeth de St Michel.

**John Pym (1584–1643)**   Leader of the Long Parliament; married Anne Hooke.

# Part I
# Analysis

# Introduction

## Early Modern Women, Sex and Gender

What did gender mean in early modern England? Historians of women and gender study a patriarchal order that is at once persistent and locally variable. Over a hundred years of research on the roles, experiences and relations of women and men in early modern England has revealed a gender hierarchy that was explicitly tied to social, political and religious stability, in which women were systematically disempowered by marriage, law, economic and social practice. Social status, age and marital status intersected with gender in fixing people's place in the order of being. Popular culture celebrated festive inversion, dramatizing reversals of hierarchy but ultimately reinscribing the established order. Alongside those structures historians have laid increasing stress on women's extensive economic and social capacity in everyday life. There were dramatic and subtle challenges to patriarchal order, such as in religious conflict, during the Civil War, and in women's collective political activism. In the wider social and religious context, a culture in which both men and women were deeply embedded in hierarchies of family and community undercuts more modern ideas of autonomy, agency and individuality. Seeing the place of gender in early modern history and ensuring that women are included in its narratives means, among other challenges, looking for the ways that 'women' were perceived as a collective group, tracing the formations of gendered roles, and analysing the power structures that differentiated people by sex alongside other distinctions.

The period 1500–1700 was a time of transformations: politically, culturally, economically and socially, a series of seismic shifts and subtler readjustments dislodged the medieval past and laid some of the foundations of the modern world. Much else about everyday life and gendered power remained basically unchanged. One of the abiding questions for historians of early modern women and gender concerns narratives of change. Early twentieth-century feminist historians often saw the late seventeenth century as the time when women lost political and economic autonomy, as the household economy expanded. Others have considered the Reformation's impact on marriage and family; the effects of the Civil War in both challenging, and ultimately reaffirming, women's traditional roles; and the rethinking of gender and family in political thought associated with the Revolution of 1688. Merry Wiesner-Hanks has argued that gender is central to the concept 'early modern', with its embedded and problematic narrative of

DOI: 10.4324/9781003090786-2

modernisation. To take three exemplary factors: social discipline, military change and global interactions were all gendered in their nature and impact, and their specific place in early modern life shaped the nature of early modern gender relations (Wiesner-Hanks, 2008). As historians have situated early modern England in the frames of the British Atlantic world, colonialism, and global history, gendered perspectives have demonstrated the centrality of gender politics to empire-building; the limits of European patriarchy; and the interwoven projects of delineating 'race' and sex.

The project of feminist and gender history reframes the subjects of history: it insists that the category of gender, with all its social, economic, religious and political ramifications, is historically changeable. Making women subjects and gender a category of analysis demands that we historicize experiences and topics that have often been treated as constant: sex, sexuality, sexual difference, family; labour relations; political citizenship. It also requires realizing the force of gender at every level of historical interpretation. Gender determined the impact of political and social changes, and as a cultural and social category, it was also subject to change itself. As rhetoric and symbol, it permeated discourses and social rituals, and as a category of power, it shaped everyday relations and lives.

Early modern discourses were peculiarly explicit about the codes of gender; the language of religion, national politics and local governance persistently connected gender order with social and religious order. Many of these rules derived from biblical and classical prescriptions, reaffirmed in the light of Protestant teaching's stress on marriage. Other features of the early modern landscape of gender were more distinctive. Anatomical sex was less clearly foundational for cultural and social gender roles than it later became, with much learned medicine still deploying a classical model of sexual difference as a spectrum, but the male body was normative and superior. Reproductive functions were a subject of discussion and discovery, in popular culture as well as elite science. Marriages were economic and social units, as well as intimate relationships. Morality was a public concern. Bodies and minds were experienced as intertwined, and individuals were embedded in networks of mutual obligations and connections. And yet, before modern understandings of sexual difference had been established, some of the conditions of modern gender relations were already in place, and the structures of gendered power were remarkably intransigent. Determining what supported and challenged them is one of the key tasks for historians of gender.

Successive waves of women's history, and more recently gender history, have examined the definitions, relations and power structures that shaped women's and men's lives in early modern England. The term 'gender', in the early modern period, referred to grammar and to generation. 'Sex' was a more familiar word, though it was applied to women – 'the female sex' – rather than to men. The distinction, important to second-wave feminism and increasingly problematic, between biological sex and cultural gender never mapped straightforwardly onto early modern medicine: sex, too, was a matter of culture. Patriarchy, an essential term of feminist analysis, is particularly useful to the early modern period, both as a generic model for gendered power, and in relation to the specific seventeenth-century political theory of patriarchalism, which symbolically linked fathers of families to heads of nations. As a social, political and economic system, patriarchy has dividends for those cast as winners – generally, men; but it also binds everyone caught in its net. Within that system, individual men could of course be subordinate to specific women, and the relations between sons and mothers, apprentices and mistresses were as significant as those between husbands and wives. So were the relations among women and among men, in which gendered power was further differentiated by rank, age and marital status. Our subjects are understood in terms of gendered norms. Masculinity and femininity are modern terms to describe these. Their closest early modern equivalents, manhood and womanhood, have associations of maturity, reflecting the way that gender roles intersected with those of age. 'Effeminate' and 'masculine' marked out the limits of gendered roles, but their implications were not the same as they are now: effeminacy suggested heterosexual excess, while masculine was not inconsistent with virtuous womanhood. The critical intersection of gender with 'race' demands a scrutiny of the languages, acts and ideas that differentiated, not just by skin colour, but by religion and national origin. The construction of gender was deeply implicated in the development and uses of racialized difference. In all these contexts, the codes of gender were sometimes explicit, and sometimes implicit: a current critical language can help illuminate them.

The history of gender relations draws on uneven sets of evidence, narratives and arguments. The recovery of women's history is an ongoing challenge. Only a small minority of women were sufficiently literate and well-resourced to write more than a few words in their own hand. Most early modern sources are not only written by (and often for) men, but when they touch on women, they are shaped by the priorities of governance and control, and often by concerns about sexual morality.

The history of men, by contrast, is ubiquitous, but it has only recently taken gender as a key focus. Part of the code of gender is that women carry it and men do not: men are the norm against which everything else is measured. Compared to the often blindingly clear rules of femininity, those of masculinity were often less immediately apparent, and they were also flexible and varied, not to mention hard to live up to. Patriarchy and masculinity are more helpfully differentiated than equated (Shepard, 2005). Scholars of sexual violence, credit, friendship and politeness have illuminated key features of early modern masculinity. The sociological concept of hegemonic masculinity has been useful in delineating the way certain qualities and achievements support men's authority: in early modern England, self-sufficiency and successful householding, including the fidelity of wives, loomed large. The economic and social pressures of the late sixteenth century left many men unable to attain those ends, resulting in competing ideas of masculinity. Early modern popular culture often makes men's power look absurdly vulnerable, at risk from the promiscuity of women, impotence and cuckoldry. Masculinity has been described as 'inherently anxious', with the orderly ideals of gender relations undercut by the difficulty of attaining secure, autonomous manhood (Breitenberg, 1996: 2). This idea can be applied both collectively, to early modern culture, and more speculatively, to individual psyches. More generally, descriptions of manhood drew heavily on dichotomies: between manliness and effeminacy, thrift and prodigality, courage and cowardice, self-governance and licence, plain-dealing and deceit. Such binaries featured in political and religious arguments across the period, reinforcing a language of divisive masculinity (Shepard, 2005).

Masculinity and femininity were both, in their different ways, unattainable ideals; men and women were both disciplined by patriarchy. Male power and authority involved not only the successful achievement of manhood, but the struggle to get there. Women's subordination, too, was produced and mediated through the interaction between precept and practice, but the room for manoeuvre was much narrower and the response to deviation from norms more punitive. The gender history of recent years has established both the power and persistence of a restrictive system, and the enterprise with which women established agency within it.

This book deals with gender relations in England between around 1500 and 1700. Neither the period nor the place should be viewed in isolation. Comparisons with Europe and Scandinavia help to elucidate the specificities of the English experience, notably a strict common law that restricted married women's legal and economic capacities. The northwestern European context had a common demographic structure in which couples married late and fairly independently. Within England, agricultural regions, legal customs and urban/rural differences had an impact on gender roles and relations. The border interactions between England, Scotland and Wales, and the colonial relationship with Ireland, were themselves constitutive of gender relations. Global connections reveal the mobility of ideas, things and people. Women and men migrated voluntarily, were transported or enslaved. On the frontiers of colonial settlement, such as in Virginia, the English encountered different systems of gender. The patriarchal ideals of early modern England were modified, challenged, sharpened and adapted in the colonial projects. Racialized slavery made capital of maternity as well as labour. English medicine, culture and society helped to create 'race' and modelled whiteness into national identity.

The chapters that follow are organized thematically around topics that are both conceptual and material. For students of the early modern period, 'women and gender' may appear as a discrete topic, or alongside 'family and marriage'. More properly both are central to the field, and gender can be a lens that transforms our understanding of past and present, and a formidable tool through which to interpret inequality, culture, belief, power and change.

# 1 Bodies and Minds

Early modern popular culture and medicine gave a distinctive form to gender, sex, body and mind. In this deeply spiritual and pre-Cartesian world, not only were the feelings and meanings of bodies and mind entwined in their meanings and feelings, but the relationship between observed anatomical difference and social or cultural gender was less secure than it became in modern medicine. Additionally, the collective, social nature of early modern communities meant that identity was primarily familial and social, private intimacy hard to find, and bodily boundaries less secure than in a more atomized society.

## Sexual Difference

Despite divides of scholarship and religion, Renaissance Europeans shared an understanding of sexual difference, derived from both biblical and classical sources, that changed little between 1500 and 1700. The physiological differences between women and men demonstrated a divine design in which the female completed the male, and was naturally inferior and subject to him. The availability of medical books in English, some written by midwives and many aimed at the ordinary reader, spread these ideas widely.

Before the Enlightenment, ordinary people's explanations of sexual difference were more likely to refer to the Bible than to biology. The creation story, as told in Genesis, underpinned female subjection by tying it not just to ethics, but to the making of male and female bodies Early modern biblical commentators and preachers noted that Eve was made *after* Adam; *from* Adam (and from his rib, not his head); and *for* Adam. The biblical narrative contained truths that applied to all humanity: all women were made for their husbands. Some of the earliest proto-feminist texts engaged with this basic argument and attempted to invert it. Jane Anger's *Protection for Women*, one of a series of defences of women in the late sixteenth and early seventeenth centuries, defended women against male slanders by redefining the creation story as one of purification, arguing that the creation of woman refined the imperfect male original [**Doc. 1**]. Dorothy Leigh's more conventional advice book, *The Mother's Blessing*, presented the Virgin Mary's labour of maternity as saving womankind from Eve's sin, a work of supreme virtue in which 'man has no part' [**Doc. 29**].

DOI: 10.4324/9781003090786-3

The inferiority of the female body was explained more fully in classical medical texts. Renaissance medicine drew deeply from ancient models; throughout the period, descriptions of sexual difference were modelled on those of **Galen** and Aristotle. The ancient model of the humoral system presented a world in which the balance of the fluids of blood, bile and phlegm, with their corresponding qualities of heat and moisture, defined or reflected temperament, complexion, age and sex. Masculinity and femininity were related to the balance in each body between hot and cold, wet and dry: heat and dryness made men, cold and wet made women. In humoral theory, physicians argued, the dry heat of men made them more prone to choler, or anger, while the cold and wet humours of women made them susceptible to melancholy [**Doc. 2**].

This model of sexual difference suggested a spectrum, with degrees of masculinity and femininity. In the teachings of Galen, the foundation for many early modern medical texts, sexed bodies were complementary: the external genitalia of the male were the equivalent of the internal genitalia of the female [**Doc. 3**]. Thomas Laqueur's influential work identifies this 'one-sex' model, with its commensurable organs and sense of sex as a spectrum, as pre-modern, predating the world of two incomparably different sexes that was constructed during the eighteenth century (Laqueur, 1990). Subsequent critiques have modified the centrality and meaning of this model. The influential Hippocratic corpus portrayed sexual difference in a diversity of ways, including by stressing menstruation as a necessary corollary of femaleness; in the seventeenth century English audiences also encountered work like that of Levinus Lemnius, in which the female body was saturated with a sexualized difference which shaped a woman's whole behaviour. Disordered wombs, the origin of hysteria, were imagined to wander, while pent-up fluids might cause fits of 'suffocation of the mother'; girls suffered green-sickness from the excess of lust before marriage [**Doc. 2**]. It has been argued that the premodern idea of sex as a spectrum of difference did not provide a solid basis for gender roles; nor did it need to, with Genesis to provide another, more pervasive, story of sexual difference. At the same time, early modern bodies were frequently depicted in terms which reinscribed male superiority, and there was already a well-established model of women's medicine based around the unique qualities of the womb.

In medical texts as elsewhere, the body was always a matter for argument and interpretation. At the popular level, varying ideas were dispersed through cheap print (such as ballads and broadsides) and oral culture. Printed medical texts repeated as orthodoxy the idea that conception required both male and female orgasm, but popular texts and everyday experience contradicted it.

Bodies were sexed in other ways than through the reproductive organs. Renaissance dramatists and satirists were fascinated by the grotesque potential of human bodies. The female body was satirized as relentlessly leaky, depicting women as susceptible to both metaphorical and literal incontinence. In popular medical books the humoral body was a semi-permeable corpus of fluids that might transform, as breast milk was composed of purified menstrual blood; when Dorothy Leigh published her maternal advice, she invoked a vision of breastfeeding in which her heart's blood rushed to nourish the child at her breast [**Doc. 27**]. Humoral theory underlined the idea of self-management, and women and men used diet, clothes and behaviour to maintain and regulate their health. The well-managed body had particular resonances for masculinity, and men's diaries show them to be preoccupied with the wayward fluids and humoral instability of wind, digestion, fits, colds and headaches. Advice to young men stressed the importance of regulation and moderation. A balanced body was the foundation of the self-control that enabled men to live up to the commanding position required of them. Humours also reflected gender, and in a world of fluid humours, weak or promiscuous men could be effeminate, and brave women manly. Extremes of female bodily behaviour fascinated audiences: fasting girls attracted attention first as miracles of spiritual self-denial and later as medical marvels.

In this largely binary world, popular and elite culture regularly referenced bodies that crossed the lines. Medical books and cheap print described 'hermaphrodites' who partook of both sexes in terms of wonder, monstrosity or both. Legal authorities explained that variant bodies would ultimately have to be assigned to one social gender. Other texts suggested ways that sexed bodies might transform themselves. In the seventeenth century some gynaecological texts began to refer to female sexual organs growing abnormally, endowing the clitoris with the potential of a man's 'yard', and enabling the lusts of 'wicked tribades' (Traub, 2002: 194). There is little evidence of how people understood gender instability in practice. But in a recently-established settlement in Virginia in 1629, Thomas Hall, from Newcastle upon Tyne, confused the community and told the plantation commander he was both man and woman; following the English habit of matronly authority, women searched him, and decided on very uncertain bodily evidence that he was a man. Thomas Hall, though, performed gender more fluidly, describing being christened Thomasine in England, adopting men's clothes later to follow a brother into the army, and then making a living sewing in women's clothes. The colonial context seems to have enforced a confrontation and Hall was ordered to wear a mix of clothes [**Doc. 4**].

Stories of corporeal transformation can also be seen as features of a landscape of gender instability or transitivity, which took various forms in the popular imaginary. Young children seemed to exist to a degree outside gender, with people often speaking of 'the child' in gender neutral terms, and dressing young boys and girls in similar garments; stricter gender roles shaped children's lives after around age seven. With masculinity sharply marked by maturity, boys could be seen as occupying a distinct gender category (Fisher, 2001). With rigidly gendered outer garments, cross-dressing in a range of contexts enabled both sexes to cross the line; on stage, boys learned gestures and poses to act women [**Doc. 10**]. Such practices and stories offered a potential transitivity or mobility to both sex and gender.

## 'Race' and Gender

Emerging discourses of 'race' intersected with those of gender. In the binary world of the early modern imaginary, 'fair' habitually denoted virtue, particularly for women, and blackness, sin. Words like tawny and nut-brown differentiated degrees of whiteness and hence status and elegance. Cosmetics painted Queen Elizabeth and her court white, assisting in the identification of feminine whiteness with purity, status, and national identity. At the Jacobean court, masques in which court ladies performed as 'blackamoors' dramatized gender, race and state power (Hall, 1996). Physicians, travel writers, and philosophers speculated whether dark skin was the result of sunburn, humours relating to the climate, or the biblical curse of Ham, and midwives' books discussed blackness in relation to myths of maternal impression, making it part of the mystery of generation; but English people, particularly but not exclusively in cities, lived alongside Africans, 'Moors' and 'Ethiops', and they saw interracial marriages.

Parish records suggest there were generally fewer Black women in England than men; around 25 per cent of the Black Londoners in parish registers of the late seventeenth century were female. Early records include the Moorish women who came in the early sixteenth-century entourage of Catherine of Aragon, the Africans living with Spanish merchants in sixteenth-century London, and a number working in textile trades, like 'Marye Phyllis a Blackamore', the daughter of a Moroccan basketmaker who worked for a London seamstress and was christened in St Botolph's Aldgate, a parish which hosted a significant Black community, in 1597 (Kaufmann, 2017). Other women were living as servants, laundresses, and occasionally working independently, part of a small, dispersed population; the servant in Figure 1.1 is thought to have been in the household of the countess of Arundel in Antwerp. From the mid-seventeenth century, Britain's growing participation in the slave trade brought enslaved people, typically young and male from West Africa, via plantations in the Caribbean and North America, and sometimes from India, to ports in London and the West Country [**Doc. 6**]. Some became free, formally, informally, or by escaping. Advertisements for runaways from this period in London newspapers describe some of those who fled. Their clothes ranged from the livery of elite servants to the smocks and gowns of household servants [**Doc. 7**]. Some were wearing brass or silver collars, marks of ownership with names engraved, that were also intended to look elegant, brutally matching those given to dogs (Newman, 2022: 120). Some had been branded on plantations and some had ritual body marks from their early years in Africa.

Writers developing ideas of otherness and race deployed gender in numerous ways. The Irish subjects of English colonial settlers were made prototypes for images of savagery: descriptions of Irish women as drunk and immodest fuelled the English project to 'civilize'. The observations of childbirth guides and travel narratives helped establish an association between the racialized other and excessive sexuality or bodily monstrosity [**Doc. 3**]. Sex, child-bearing and child-raising practices were all used to mark indigenous women out: sometimes as natural mothers or exceptionally modest, increasingly as different and beastly, and finally as a productive, reproductive resource (Morgan, 1997). Imagining Black women was integral to the projects of race, labour, and empire.

*Figure 1.1* Portrait of an African woman by Wenceslaus Hollar, 1645. Possibly done in
Antwerp, where the woman may have been a member of the household of
Althea Talbot, Countess of Arundel, as Hollar was. Etching, 62 × 46 cm.
© Rijksmuseum, Amsterdam, The Netherlands/Bridgeman Images.

## The Social Body

The experience of embodiment was historically and socially variable. Mortality
rates were differentiated by sex, with women at high risk in the childbearing
years, although if they survived those years, their life expectancy exceeded
men's. Workplace accidents plagued both sexes. The close work of sewing or
lace-making made eye problems especially likely for women. After a lifetime of
physical labour, old age was felt sharply: the effects of menopause, such as
decreased bone density and malnutrition were likely to give older women a
distinctive look, familiar in popular images of witches. Old age gave to men an
authority that did not accrue to women: their knowledge of custom made them
key informants in parish affairs, especially if they could lay claim to a chain
of memories from their fathers or other old men. But the effects of injury,

debilitation and consequent loss of livelihood left many men as reduced in status as women, and past the peak of masculine achievement, old age, which could begin around 50, may have had a levelling effect. By the precepts of humoral medicine, old men were liable to melancholy as their hot, dry humours were sunk by the chilling process of ageing, bringing them closer to the natural temperaments of women. Old age also brought single men and women together in labour relationships: poor women's nursing and washing work kept many old men going.

The body was an instrument of social as well as sexual relations. Dense family and social structures were mirrored in a lack of privacy and, in some contexts at least, high levels of physical contact. Elite status provided distance and space, especially for men; increasingly great houses included closets for personal reflection. Plebeian women and men lived closely, with little separate space, rooms that opened into each other without corridors, and minimal privacy. Bed-sharing with others of the same sex was common in ordinary and elite households, between parents and children, masters or mistresses and servants, tutors and students, and domestic servants or apprentices. A pragmatic practice, it could also be a gesture of solidarity and favour.

Early modern people took care with their gestures. Manhood was perceived to involve self-control, but male tears were also sometimes engagingly appropriate (Capp, 2014). Rituals of shared drinking cemented social and economic relationships. With the expansion of the market, credit depended on careful assessment of a new colleague's trustworthiness: bodily presentation was bound to matter. Drinking healths was the epitome of good (male) fellowship, and it sealed contracts and resolved disputes. While women used alehouses for business purposes too, their participation in these kinds of rituals seems to have been limited to betrothals. Contemporary manners advice addressed itself largely to children, but was most specific about the behaviour of boys in training to be gentlemen. The art of impressing others was understood to be crucial to self-advancement, especially in the city or at court. In the late seventeenth-century politeness became a key indicator of status and respectable manhood, while violence was less commonly used to sort out men's disputes (Shoemaker, 1999).

In the rhetoric of early modern demeanour, public behaviour was not just a performance, but a mirror of the man within. Hat honour, bowing and handshaking all changed their meaning and their uses across different contexts and over time. Katherine Austen's angry outburst directs itself at her son's failure to raise his hat: the contemporary fashion of his largely male collegiate world, meant to her, in a city of merchants and lawyers, arrogance and lack of gentility [Doc. 8].

The rules of public behaviour were less explicit for women: the central image of their good manners was that of 'honest carriage', and while the cosmetics, light feet and lack of humility that distinguished a light carriage were frequently commented on, the characteristics of an honest woman were much harder to pinpoint. Avoiding direct eye contact was one demonstration of chastity. There were, however, explicit rules for some at the margins. The poor women who searched bodies for signs of plague were ordered to walk by the gutter, carrying red wands, to segregate them from the other users of the public street [**Doc. 35**].

In the mid-seventeenth century, differing political and religious identities were reflected in novel bodily styles. The political cataclysms of the Civil War years were played out through two distinctive masculine presentations: Roundheads and Cavaliers each had gendered modes of comportment and dress. One group, the Quakers, broke all the rules of comportment in refusing to doff their hats as a mark of respect, and treating all people, radically, as social equals.

## Clothes and Hair

Clothes helped make gender. The majority of the population owned few garments, and changed them infrequently. Especially in the sixteenth century, clothes were made to last and were often inherited or purchased second-hand, with women playing a prominent role in the market. Passing on used clothes was part of the informal contract between employers and servants. Men and women were recognizable by the shape of their outer garments: petticoats, waistcoats, gowns and coats. Inner garments, particularly the linen smocks that everyone wore, were more gender-neutral, and with shared sleeping arrangements and infrequent bathing, were almost like a second skin. Small children's status as less clearly gendered than adults was symbolized in the long gowns that both boys and girls wore until boys were 'breeched' at around seven years old. In a gentry household of the seventeenth century, Frank North's grandmother supervised his transition into breeches and long coats, recording his excitement for his absent father. Equally significant for the newly made boy and his family was the reaction of the minister, who, surprised at seeing him in his new clothes, was 'put to the blush'. Adult dress marked the transition of a young boy towards his place in the governing class [**Doc. 9**].

Girls' transition to the next stage of maturity was marked, less publicly, by starting to wear boned bodices. This was common practice for young girls of the elite in the earlier seventeenth century, and among the middling sort by the mid-century. A more momentous change for young women came when they covered their heads as adults or wives. A coif and sometimes also a hat over the hair was the sign of marriage and respectability: at weddings and funerals, single women left their hair uncovered to mark their maidenhood, though as the seventeenth century progressed, they increasingly covered their heads with scarves and hats at other times. Head coverings for women were also a mark of modesty and subjection, and it was perhaps for that reason that, in New England, the flexibly gendered Thomas/ine Hall was ordered to wear them, with an apron, alongside men's clothes [**Doc 4**]. For men, beards were an important marker of masculinity, denoting both maturity and martial vigour. Medical writers attributed men's capacity to grow beards to the strength of male seed; some argued shaving the chin made men womanish. Weapons were another, more divisive, emblem of manhood: elite men carried swords and daggers;

constables' honorary authority was symbolized in their staves. In images and in life, gender, status and age were identifiable by transferrable attributes.

In the high fashion of Elizabethan and Stuart England, clothes displayed gendered style for both women and men. Elaboration and flamboyance were hallmarks of male style, from the elongated codpieces of the sixteenth century to the wide breeches and garnishing ribbons of the 1660s. Both sexes were regularly castigated by moralists, especially by Puritans, for excessive adornment, waste of fabric and displays of pride. Men's clothes accentuated the public significance of sexual potency. Codpieces grew larger and larger under Henry VIII and fell out of fashion by the reign of Elizabeth; at the turn of the century men's fashions featured padded hose and pointed doublets that made the male body look markedly more feminine. In the mid-seventeenth century reforming Protestants distinguished themselves by quiet, dark dress with plain linen collars. Their opposition to fashion created a Puritan style in itself, one which became emblematic of the politics of sobriety and reform in contrast to the loose, half-unbuttoned doublets of 'cavaliers'. The allegation of effeminacy sometimes levelled at men's garments had a different meaning in this period than it would do in later centuries. Effeminacy came from too much contact with women, and too much (heterosexual) sex; it might undermine male authority, but it did not necessarily imply homosexuality.

Women's high fashion was as elaborate as men's and as sexually charged. Ruffs and loose doublets, in fashion in the early seventeenth century, were frequently attacked as evidence of pride; perfumed gloves, velvet face masks and beauty spots, cosmetics and headdresses were all described as deceitful masks. More than men, women were accused of counterfeiting social status with dress, causing a confusion of categories – prostitutes with gentlewomen, pretentious poor with bourgeoisie. Accessories such as gloves carried rich significance, especially when given as gifts to women. Busks, the stiff front sections of corsets, were sometimes gifted with erotic or loving inscriptions, suggesting an array of meanings by which men might stake a claim to women through material objects (Bendall, 2014). More practically, women's garments might add risk, constraint or pragmatism to the conditions of daily life and work. Hanging pockets provided extensive capacity for carrying money, keys, and for some, stolen goods. Englishwomen's habit of not wearing drawers was both practical and risky. The pins that held garments together could be improvised as self-defence; plebeian rural women were also, like men, likely to be carrying small knives.

Clothes were the lineaments of social identity. Joris Hoefnagel's painting of a Bermondsey wedding or fete (Figure 1.2) features a number of interesting vignettes: two women with masculine hats, perhaps incorporating male dress into the festivities; a mother or wet-nurse using a rich red shawl or coat to carry a baby she is breastfeeding; and women wearing aprons outside. Elizabethan England still had sumptuary laws, which prescribed who was allowed to wear velvet, silk, and taffeta, and a woman's apparel was meant to match her husband's status. By the late sixteenth century, sumptuary laws were less binding on fashion, but the fabrics and shape of clothes continued to be the subject of controversy.

*Figure 1.2 A Fete at Bermondsey* by Joris Hoefnagel (1542–1600). Oil on panel, *c.*1570, 73.8 × 99 cm.
Wikimedia Commons, public domain.

With a relatively rigid distinction between male and female garments, cross-dressing was a significant feature of popular culture. Some women dressed as men to follow husbands or lovers into military service, or to make a man's living; some were discovered as 'female husbands' after marrying women. The stories and plays about Moll Cutpurse were based on a real woman, prosecuted for dressing in men's clothes to pick pockets and go to plays. For some, cross-dressing was a protection or disguise, its employment revealing how differently women and men passed through the streets, particularly at night. Mawdlin Gawen, one of a series of women arrested and sent to London's Bridewell prison for wearing men's clothes, described how she had disguised herself to keep her meetings with her lover secret [**Doc. 10**]. In the legal records, overlaps between prostitution, illicit sex and cross-dressing suggest erotic meanings as well as pragmatism. Stories of men dressing as women to deceive are, in contrast, very rare.

Fashion toyed with subtler cross-dressings. Two pamphlets of the 1620s, *Hic Mulier* and *Haec Vir*, deliberately mismatched Latin gendered pronouns to complain of women and men adopting each other's styles; they were talking not about breeches or skirts, but doublets, ruffs, and short hair, the same fashions that James I had urged his clergy to attack earlier that year [**Doc. 11**]. Women in men's fashions, *Hic Mulier* suggests, might acquire men's prerogatives of violence and assertiveness, as well as becoming dangerously lewd. Androgyny was a touchpaper for lust. The extremes of gendered fashion were also debated in the years leading up to the Civil War: satire and news highlighted women who looked or acted like men, men who appeared effeminate, and the link between certain fashions and 'popery'.

Finally, the gendered meanings of clothing include the labour by which women made and remade the detachable elements of everyday wear and high fashion. While tailoring was widely understood as a male prerogative, the provision and cleaning of linen such as smocks, drawers, ruffs and bands was women's responsibility, overlapping with the provision of nappies, bandages and menstrual rags.

## Sexuality

Early modern popular culture was often bawdy, replete with sexual metaphor. Jokes and proverbs about sex abounded, giving people a language in which to imagine and critique sexual relations and morality. The political tracts of the civil war period, liberated from print censorship, sometimes featured sexual satires and gossip. Pornography – literally, writing about prostitutes, which was the nature of most early pornography – was available first in manuscript, and by the 1660s in print in Latin, French and English. The evidence of jest-books suggests a verbal compass for women that was much wider than that prescribed in advice for virtuous conduct: old women, wives, widows and maidens were both subjects and speakers of bawdy humour [**Doc. 12**].

Sex outside marriage was powerfully proscribed. The **church courts** enforced a canon law which prohibited sex before marriage, and made adultery a cause for separation (although not remarriage); family, neighbours and parish **constables** enforced moral rules with the surveillance of a closely knit community, in which women took a significant role as moral arbiters. The articles of complaint presented against one couple in Worcester in the 1660s presented a list of issues which focused on illicit sex, but also encompassed the man's rejection of his wife, his widowed lover's disrespect of the mother she lived with, and the rumour that she was either pregnant or had procured an abortion [**Doc. 13**]. Privacy was not easy to achieve in most rural or urban surroundings, as Mawdlin Gawen's disguises and pretences reveal [**Doc. 10**].

Hardest to recapture through the partial records of sexual encounters is the history of desire, pleasure and power. Renaissance literature cast women as naturally lustful, with overwhelming desires, but the cultural landscape also featured a classical model of men as forceful warriors on the battlefield of sex and love. Leonard Wheatcroft's courtship narrative tells a story precisely in this mould [**Doc. 14**]. Male diarists, notably **Samuel Pepys**, occasionally left some evidence: Pepys's diary records insistent sexual pursuit, persuasion and harassment of the women he met in his daily life. Female writers, all of them elite, left almost no discussion of sex. This lack reflects not just inhibition, but a constrained language, and a set of narratives and metaphors for sex that persistently cast women and men in predictable scripts. Some of the most explicit descriptions of sex by women come from legal records of bastardy and fornication, such as that of

Elizabeth Browne in early seventeenth-century Somerset. Not surprisingly, such accounts make men the pursuers, women the passive accomplices or victims: men invariably 'take the pleasure of' or 'occupy' them, although this story also interestingly begins with some sense of wooing words and gestures [Doc. 15]. This sense of female lack of agency was reinforced by the descriptions in anatomical texts of women as passive and receptive, men as active. Meanwhile the idea that women required pleasure to conceive may have legitimated female sexuality, but it also provided fuel for misogynist fantasies and political parodies like the 'Parliament of Women' whose members demanded nothing but more sex. Despite all this, in scraps of conversation reported in court and in their letters, there is some evidence of women's ownership of their desires and a determination to act on them.

Knowledge about reproduction was contentious and guarded, kept particularly from the young and single. Vernacular medical books had begun to appear in the late sixteenth century, outlining the genital parts and their functions, so that a careful reader could easily put together clues about the management of fertility (and hence contraception). Masturbation went largely unmentioned until eighteenth-century texts, focusing on men, started to describe it as sinful. In the pursuit of successful conception, the late seventeenth century popular guide to reproduction, *Aristotle's Masterpiece*, also offered a chapter on how men should ensure the sexual pleasure of their female partners. Works like this functioned as erotic as well as educational, and alongside them was a bawdy popular culture and a manuscript, later print, repertoire of early pornography.

Most medical literature told readers that conception required seed, and thus orgasm, from both male and female partners [Doc. 3]. Not until the early twentieth century was the particular operation of human ovulation understood. The implications of this view of conception were important, even if it countered what many people must have learnt from experience. Women were understood to need sexual fulfilment: the result of postponing marriage too long could be chlorosis, or greensickness, a disease of melancholy that was peculiar to women. A joke ascribed to Nicholas L'Estrange's mother mocks a young maid who could not wait for marriage to satisfy her desires [Doc. 12].

Women's lust, then, was natural, which is not to say that it was tolerated; rather, women were seen as particularly likely to sin. Despite the growing stress on male continence after the Reformation, when Protestants and especially **Puritans** stressed the significance of sexual fidelity to marriage, women continued to bear the brunt of sexual blame. In 1650, following the longstanding aims of some Puritans, Cromwell's government reformed the laws on adultery, incest, and fornication to bring them firmly within the compass of secular law. Adultery, which became a capital offence, was redefined, based on **Mosaic law** in the Bible, as sex with a married woman; men could be prosecuted, but it was the woman who was understood to be most firmly bound by marriage, and sex between a single woman and a married man was not adultery, but fornication, punished by imprisonment. Actual prosecutions under this act very largely targeted women, though few were convicted and there is barely any evidence of executions. The Commonwealth government had presented itself effectively as the upholder of rigid sexual discipline. While some cases were actually prompted by women's complaints against their husbands' infidelity, both women and men articulated satirical and heartfelt opposition to its brutality (Hughes 2011: 137–8).

The late seventeenth century saw a shift in attitudes, with moral regulation increasingly hard to enforce. The church courts, in hiatus during the civil wars, were no longer sufficiently robust to monitor everyday sexual behaviour, and neighbours were less ready to prosecute each other. In London and major cities, the campaigns of the **Societies for the Reformation of Manners** pressed for brief, draconian clampdowns on fornication and sodomy, but the viability of sexual policing was dramatically reduced. By necessity, illicit sex was more likely to be tolerated, and it began to be perceived, at least in some circumstances, as a private matter. The power of sexual shame for women remained significant.

The extent of illegitimacy provides some evidence for sexual practices. From 1538 onwards, there are fairly dependable records of births outside marriage. Rates of illegitimacy were surprisingly low, particularly for a pre-industrial society with late marriage. Between 2 and 4 per cent of all births over the period were illegitimate, equating to roughly 8–16 per cent of *first* births. On top of this, 16 and 25 per cent of first children were born fewer than nine months after their parents' marriage, suggesting a marriage pattern that was led by courtship and sometimes prompted by pregnancy. In the sixteenth century spousals, or contracts, were still often a precursor to marriage, and sex after the contract was understood to make it binding. Regional variations also indicate higher levels of births outside marriage in more loosely governed areas of pastoral farming and textile industry, in the north, west and southwest of the country, and lower levels in the more closely settled arable areas of the lowland southeast, where social control seems to have been stronger.

One of the significant cultural changes of this period related to sexual violence. In medieval England, rape had been a property offence: it concerned the abduction of a young woman from her guardians, and it was prosecuted by her father or brother. In the sixteenth century it was classed with theft and murder as a capital offence without **benefit of clergy**; as with other offences, its severity made it hard to convict. But in the seventeenth century it became more clearly perceived as a sexual crime, and one in which the behaviour of the victim was critical. She was required to make hue and cry, and to prove her lack of consent [**Doc. 16**]. Pregnancy could potentially undermine a rape story, as conception was thought to require pleasure. The dangers of men committing rape were widely acknowledged, but it was not until the late seventeenth century that violent lust and libertinage began to feature in masculinity. While rape was viewed with concern and severity, the complexities of evidence in a legal system requiring witness evidence were widely understood to impede successful prosecution. The challenge of bringing a case was particularly large for single women whose honour was at issue. Most cases of sexual violence, of course, never received any legal consideration.

The close study of language has enhanced our understanding of what rape and consent meant to men and women. The available terminology for describing rape, at least in law, was as limited as the opportunity to prosecute it: typically, women described their clothes being torn, their possessions destroyed, rather than articulate what had been done to their bodies. The typical phraseology for sex of men 'occupying', or more formally 'having the carnal knowledge of', put women already in the passive voice; the place for discussing active desire and consent was hard to find.

Sex for money ranged from informal, occasional exchanges to a quite structured system of prostitution involving bawds and bawdy houses in London. Until the 1530s, a community of women, many of whom were Flemish, worked as prostitutes on the south bank of the Thames, with their own rules and codes of dress. The trade was tolerated on condition it was contained within 'bawdy houses'. Henry VIII's reformation abolished the zone of tolerance, and by the late sixteenth century brothels were more dispersed across London, clustered particularly in the suburban area of Clerkenwell. Attempts to prosecute prostitutes, and less effectively their clients, reached a peak in the late sixteenth century. The official campaigns were accompanied by attacks by apprentices, traditionally the city's rioters; the licence they were traditionally given effectively authorized assaults by young men on sexually active women. The 'bawdy house riots' of 1668 revisited the ancient tradition, women again the targets.

Historians of sexuality stress the distinctiveness of the premodern sexual regime, arguing that whereas modern sexuality often focuses on identities, premodern thinking revolved around acts. Heterosexuality and homosexuality are modern concepts, defined in the nineteenth century to comprise and medicalize an identity. In the early modern period sexual acts between two people of the same sex may have been criminal but they were not inconsistent with marriage and heterosexuality, and typically same-sex sex had implications for gender, rather than sexuality. Sodomy was understood to be an unnatural crime, targeted by Henry VIII's revision of canon law. It was a capital offence that, as far as we know from limited records, was infrequently prosecuted, and unlike the occasional case in Europe, it did not legally include women. While the sodomite was pilloried (literally so in the prosecutions of the late seventeenth century), in daily life homosociality was fundamental to masculine bonding, with shared beds and close physical contact both practical and a sign of esteem. One point of convergence of these understandings of relations between men came at the Jacobean court, where James I's succession of favourites put love between men at the heart of political favour [**Doc. 17**].

At the end of our period the sexual regime changed. In the transformed urban world of London, a public culture of homosexuality, with recognizable meeting places and habits, appeared and it was targeted by prosecutions and public exposures. By the eighteenth century pamphlets and ballads described 'molly houses' depicting a shared culture and community of men seeking sex with each other, and suggesting at least some of the elements of modern 'sexuality' were present. Sex between women, in contrast, was treated more discreetly, partly because it was not explicitly criminalized. In an unusual law-suit in 1680, Arabella Hunt sought to have her marriage to Amy Pulter dis-solved: the grounds were not lesbianism but bigamy, and Pulter, who had presented herself (in jest, she claimed) as a man, was asked if she was 'of a double gender' (Mendelson and Crawford, 1995). Alongside the tales of mar-riages of two women which appeared in popular culture, lesbian sex featured explicitly throughout the seventeenth century in erotic and medical texts. Leo Africanus's tales of Africa described Moroccan witches as 'fricatrices', who lured women from their husbands; alongside these tales were descriptions of male innkeepers who dressed as women, and women who were absurdly pam-pered by their husbands. This reportage fitted into a larger picture of making gender disorder at once erotic and foreign [**Doc. 5**]. Racialization was also at play: a series of stories and citations referenced women in Egypt and else-where – always far from 'here' – who used their clitorises to please other women. In 1708, rumours that Queen Anne's courtier and favourite, **Abigail Masham**, preferred to spend her nights with women rather than men were clearly understood.

## Reproduction

The printed literature of the sixteenth century onwards bears witness to a determined attempt to make sense of reproduction, or 'generation', one of early modern science's great mysteries. The 'secrets of women' were unfolded in large and small vernacular books with vivid illustrations of reproductive organs, first by men, and by the later seventeenth century by midwives.

The discovery of eggs in the follicles of women's ovaries, and sperm in the semen of men, provided evidence that would eventually transform the under-standing of reproduction. But in the shorter term generation remained a subject of debate. Preformationists believed the foetus was already present before con-ception in sperm or eggs, requiring only to be nourished; Aristotelians thought menstrual blood was the nourishing fluid that made life out of seed. Inter-pretations varied as to whether women and men were equal partners in the business of generation, whether women's role was passively to nurture the seed that men actively produced, or whether women's eggs in fact contained the miniature of new life, to be breathed into existence by sperm. Such contests had obvious implications for gender politics and the meaning of paternity.

Contraception was scarce and ineffective. Ovulation and the timing of ferti-lity were not yet correctly identified. Withdrawal was surely used, but is rarely mentioned. Breastfeeding seems to have worked fairly effectively to prevent pregnancy, as women who were undernourished and fed their babies on demand were likely to find their periods were delayed in returning. There was a widespread awareness of the most popular means of abortion, the herb savin or pennyroyal [**Doc. 13**]. Those who did not know about it probably knew someone else – a cunning-woman, an older friend or a herbalist – to ask for advice.

In a nation collectively concerned about low birth rates and healthy reproduction, potency and fertility were much discussed. Infertility was not perceived as an exclusively female problem, but attracted remedies that ranged from the magical to the practical. Fertility was a matter of public discussion, and female expertise; when Samuel and Elizabeth Pepys could not conceive, he took advice from their married women friends [**Doc. 18**].

Childbirth in early modern England was a time of magic and danger, and it took place largely in a world of women. The reproductive process involved transformations within the mysterious female body. Seeds met to make a foetus, which grew to maturity; menstrual blood was converted to breast milk; in popular lore every choice a mother-to-be made, from food to entertainment, could affect her child [**Doc. 3; Doc. 19**]. Such ideas, from the medical to the folkloric, made women easy to blame, and marginalized men from pregnancy. This was reflected in the practicalities of pregnancy and childbirth management, and in the fears of witchcraft causing miscarriage or children's deaths. The precarious time of labour and delivery was surrounded by rituals carefully prescribed to ensure safety, secrecy and nurture. While the actual levels of maternal mortality were relatively low, death in childbirth was a fear for almost every woman who wrote about it. Child mortality was high. Around one child in four died before the age of one, and another one in four before the age of ten.

Magical and folk beliefs provided ways of keeping the vulnerable woman and her child safe. Traditional childbirth remedies included girdles that had been wrapped around a statue of the Virgin Mary, necklaces and saints' relics. While Protestant reformers tried to discourage and prevent 'superstitious' rituals, women continued to use magical and sympathetic objects. One of these, the 'eagle stone', a stone within a stone, symbolized the pregnant body; it could both keep the foetus safely in the womb, or tied to the thigh, could encourage it to move down ready for delivery. Births were attended usually by a midwife and perhaps other friends, relatives or neighbours; windows and doors were closed to keep the room warm and protected from evil influences. After the birth the newly-delivered mother and her companions, the gossips, shared a specially made warm drink, caudle, of beer or wine mixed with eggs and sugar. Childbirth was a time when women from different social ranks might mix: visiting the local women lying-in belonged to a gentlewoman's duties. It was a time where women collected, briefly, in a segregated world, excluding the single (usually) and men (almost always). This might bring a degree of female empowerment, with the recently delivered woman protected, fed and nurtured by her family and friends. Ralph Josselin's diary records the close neighbourly hospitality that, along with divine mercy, protected his wife [**Doc. 20**].

Through and after the Reformation, the rituals surrounding childbirth were politically and religiously charged. The use of gossips became, for Puritans, symbolic of old superstitions; the ceremonies of the Commonwealth saw some women following 'the new way' of baptizing without gossips. The month of childbirth and lying-in culminated in another controversial ceremony.

Churching, the ceremony that marked the end of lying-in and the reintegration of the new mother into her community, had originally been a ritual of cleansing: the woman was sometimes sprinkled with holy water and wore a white veil, as the priest accompanied her into the church. Despite the 1552 *Book of Common Prayer*'s replacement of the term purification with thanksgiving or churching, for some Protestants churching retained elements of its Jewish origins, superstition and popery. The veil symbolized this, and in some cases women, or ministers, refused it for doctrinal reasons. The feasting that surrounded the ceremony also roused concerns, and it was of course closed to single mothers. Jane Minors of Barking was multiply at fault, for failing to have her child baptized, and also for coming to be churched with the wrong attitude [**Doc. 22**]. The vast majority of women continued to be churched. A ceremony that seemed to be a punitive representation of the post-partum body and a way of disciplining women could also fulfil important needs and continued to do so into the twentieth century.

Reproduction was women's business but it was also a public affair. The degree to which women controlled the realm of childbirth gave them authority both in the household, and in the community. Far from being suspected of witchcraft, midwives acted as authoritative community figures; they were more likely to search suspected women, than to be targeted themselves. The published books by midwives of the seventeenth century insisted on their knowledge and expertise, which contributed to Enlightenment science. From the mid-seventeenth century, male physicians' doubts about female knowledge contested midwives' understandings, but while male midwives gained a gradual following among elite women, most women were still delivered by other women. Until the medicalization of childbirth and the use of hospitals for giving birth, childbirth remained a largely female arena. The politics of reproduction made it fertile ground for gender conflicts.

## Mind and Soul

In humoral theory and in the popular mentality, body and mind were intimately related. The humours that determined bodily complexion also reflected temperaments: choleric, melancholic, sanguine and phlegmatic. It could thus be argued that women and men were naturally prone to certain physical and mental behaviours. The association of choler with masculinity naturalized male violence and associated it with virtuous courage; the corollary was that women's anger was rare and unnatural. Melancholy, associated with the cold, damp humour of femininity, was characteristically female. Emotions and events were understood to have corporeal sequelae, with envy, love and rage, like the longings of pregnancy, doing things to the body.

Among the literate, the habit of self-reflection was facilitated by Protestantism, by literacy and by reading. Throughout the period, literacy was sharply gendered, though writing was likely more differentiated than reading, which was learned earlier. By 1600, yeomen and tradesmen and craftsmen were increasingly able to sign their names; their wives and daughters still mostly were not. Urban life, with all the cultural capital it gave to writing and reading and the educational opportunities for girls and boys, made a considerable difference. The sheer amount of cheap print in circulation, particularly in the 1640s and 1650s, suggests reading literacy was high among both sexes.

Educational opportunities were differentiated by gender. The humanist reformation of education in the sixteenth century turned elite boys' education towards independence and the development of the faculties for governing: for girls, virtue, self-occupation and restraint remained the aspiration. Among the elites, both boys and girls began with tutors or governesses, and boys later left for tutoring away from home, school and sometimes university; girls were also sent away, but into other elite households to learn social more than intellectual skills. Not until the early seventeenth century did boarding schools for girls appear in London and other cities and towns, and their curricula continued to focus on domestic affairs, needlework and music. By the late seventeenth century, though, a few writers on girls' education were recognizing the need for some to be able to earn, and the function of education broadened somewhat. The long career of a middling status London woman, Bathsua Makin, illustrates something of the transition. Born in the early seventeenth century and educated herself by a schoolteacher father, she was rich in classical and modern languages, and after her marriage was employed to teach Princess Elizabeth, daughter of Charles I. By the 1670s, she was offering astronomy, physic, experimental philosophy and a wide range of languages to gentlemen's daughters at her boarding school in Tottenham High Cross, something which would have been unimaginable in her youth [Doc. 23].

In Renaissance thinking masculinity was habitually associated with reason and self-control, which enabled men to master both themselves and others; femininity could be correlated with unreason and passion, the lower self ruling the higher. Hysteria and greensickness symbolized the erratic control women had over their physical selves and their minds, and particularly the power and dangers of sexual desire and the reproductive process.

Against these constructs of femininity, from the late sixteenth century onwards printers published tracts in defence of the female sex, some written by real women and some pseudonymous or uncertain, often entwined with political or religious critiques which used gender politics as an emblem of other hierarchies. All assisted in establishing a collective female voice. Texts such as Jane Anger's drew on the discipline of rhetoric to identify and resist the obstacles created by representations of women as sexualized, irrational and unchaste [Doc. 1]. Until the late seventeenth century, debates about the nature and role of women ran on familiar and largely rhetorical lines. Rather than imagining a world of equality, they argued over the comparative virtues of women and men, using biblical and classical examples. The potential for feminist argument was constrained by the relationship between household and state, and by national and religious politics which predicated order on female subordination. The late seventeenth century saw a shift, with educated women arguing for women's learning and for their equal capacity. Judith Drake's *Essay in Defence of the Female Sex* drew on the force of reason and the discoveries of medical science to demonstrate that women's inferiority was entirely social and educational [**Doc. 24**]. Yet Tory royalists like Drake and Mary Astell also maintained the importance of wives obeying husbands as subjects did monarchs. In debates like this, comparisons with women's role elsewhere in Europe, particularly Holland, helped early modern writers and readers conceptualize the provisionality of gender roles.

While access to publishing was uneven, the intellectual world of early modern women with money and education was expansive, supported by letter-writing, manuscript circulation, wide reading, and experiment. The speculative world of early Enlightenment science involved women at the margins, notably Margaret Cavendish, the first woman to attend a meeting of the Royal Society (in 1667); she criticized the use of microscopy, partly from her own familiarity with the instruments, and her individuality or eccentricity brought her into conflict. Elsewhere, women involved themselves in the study of 'natural philosophy', the investigation of metals through alchemy, domestic experimentation and medical recipes. Recent scholarship has stressed the importance of the kitchen and the home as a sphere of investigation; recipe books, of which many survive, were not just for cooking but for medical experimentation. Empirical knowledge was increasingly valued, and women had practical expertise, particularly in domestic medicine. Many women kept fully up to date with scientific developments, and the study of astronomy and geography was particularly popular in the seventeenth century. It was the formalization of scientific experiment in the later seventeenth century that marginalized women, as natural philosophy became science, demonstrated with public display and masculine networking.

At the end of the seventeenth century, another strain in the development of the self can be traced: politeness provided a model for men to aspire to and women to judge. The 'man of feeling' who modelled a certain kind of masculinity in the eighteenth century could trace some roots back to the late seventeenth-century middling sort's urban world of sociability and intellectual exchange, in which sentiment, self-consciousness and reflection shaped the self.

By the end of the seventeenth century, the natural foundation of both patriarchy and inequality could no longer always be taken for granted. But challenges to them were still bound by the necessity of political and social obedience.

## Spirituality

The Protestant Reformation opened the possibility of a soul free from the constraints of earthly gender. The doctrine of the priesthood of all believers suggested the potential of both women and men to interpret God's word for themselves. Theologians agreed that there was no division of the sexes in the immortal world; the disabilities of femininity were earthbound. But there were different images of male and female believers. Both Catholic and Protestant teachings asserted that women were naturally more pious than men, with piety associated with obedience and silence. The female worshipper was often seen as a passive vessel. Reformers in England and Europe expressed concerns about women, especially servants, reading and discussing the Bible without proper supervision to prevent dangerous misinterpretation; in 1543 Henry VIII's *Act for the Advancement of the True Religion* prohibited women, along with journeymen and those under the rank of yeomen, from reading the Bible either openly or in private. Anne Boleyn and Catherine Parr, however, both engaged heavily in scriptural interpretation and discussion of religious reforms.

Historians have disagreed on the extent to which Protestant reforms had a gender-specific impact. The broader effect of Protestantism on gender relations is particularly hard to judge in England, where the Reformation happened slowly and piecemeal. In part this debate follows the sharp divisions of Reformation historiography in relation to popular religious devotions, the role of saints in late medieval Catholicism, and the advent of a more Christocentric religion. Revisionist historians of the Reformation have stressed its dramatic break from the medieval church; the rejection of the cult of saints, and in particular their intercessory powers, would have had profound consequences, and the emphasis on Christ rather than Mary and the many female saints suggest particular consequences for women's devotions. Others have pointed out the continuities. Christine Peters sees the shift towards Christocentric piety as already under way in the late medieval period, and points out the risks of 'biological essentialism' in making assumptions about women's use of female saints (Peters, 2003). In an analysis of the reproductive politics of the Reformation, Mary Fissell observes the ways that Protestant thought reconfigured the female reproductive body. Henry VIII's bishops targeted childbirth rituals, destroying the cherished relics that were lent to women in labour and banning thank-offerings to the Virgin. Argument about the role and significance of the Virgin Mary included the question of her contribution to his human form, and the impact of bearing Christ on Mary's body: in 1536 a preacher in Kent allegedly compared her to a saffron bag. The belief that Mary's body only held the faint trace of holiness after Christ was born, 'like a bag of saffron or pepper when the spice was out', was specifically proscribed by the Church that year: it was clearly a potent simile (Fissell 2004: 55). Joan Bocher, accused of heresy in the 1540s, expressed the conviction that Mary had two kinds of seed, corporeal and heavenly, the latter responsible for the conception of Christ. Thus the descriptions in anatomical books, with their varying interpretations of the miraculous process of conception, could carry doctrinal significance.

While some women participated in outright conflict, such as the Pilgrimage of Grace, and were martyred for public dissent, the sixteenth century also presented many opportunities for tacit religious resistance. Catholic women under Protestant regimes helped shelter priests and provided domestic support for a beleaguered religion. Rose Hickman, in exile under Mary I, found ways to resist the Catholic rituals associated with baptism [**Doc. 25**]. John Foxe's *Book of Martyrs*, reprinted through the period, featured models of more explicit female resistance, alongside men. Foxe's female martyrs were noted for their resistance, constancy, masculine courage and often, their wit. Many of his women refuse to obey their husbands, leave their family homes and work, and resist worldly authorities. While the model of simple, uneducated women provides a convenient image of the weaker vessels God uses to perform great things, Foxe's women are also often witty, cunning and dazzling interlocutors, silencing their baffled interrogators. Alice Driver, in Foxe's account, caused her interrogator to give up and put his head down on a pillow [**Doc. 26**]. The humility of poor women, whose education was apparently confined to deep reading of (or listening to) the Bible, stood in sharp contrast to the subtleties of the men trying to convict them. Some of these accounts were based on records from the trials; others may have been elaborated as they were passed on. But they put a surprising variety of models for women's resistance at the heart of a core text of Protestant identity, leaving a long legacy. Catholics noted the dangers of domestic disorder from the early days of Reformation teaching, but women's resistance to conforming husbands was also a feature of Catholic martyr narratives.

For men, Protestant theology opened another possibility: clerical marriage and sexuality. No longer did clerical life require a commitment to celibacy. The married clergy of the Reformation years broke new ground in leading family lives that were meant to be exemplary rather than regrettable. The household was the place for establishing and reproducing the new religion. The clerical wives of that generation made a new position for themselves too.

Puritanism had its own gender order. Its stress on active citizenship gave spiritual significance to the growing opportunities for civic authority available to middling sort men, while the conflict of disorderly or lewd women with Puritan magistrates was a stock archetype of the period. The personal devotions of Puritan women were a spur to reflective writing and sometimes to prophecy. Puritan theology included the duty of obedience and humility, which fitted neatly with women's natural obligation to their husbands; it could also authorize resistance and actions of conscience, with the refusal to follow established rituals. Godly women were stock characters in the discourse of seventeenth-century spirituality. While some ministers praised their conformity and godliness, others attacked their insubordinate zeal, and warned of the danger of women evading the divine headship of men. The stock images of gossips, shrews and harlots were augmented by depictions of zealous arguers, whose roots can be traced in the proud, stubborn women of Foxe's martyrology.

The autonomous spirituality that is often seen as typically Protestant was by no means uniquely male; women's devotions offered a space for intellectual reflection that was rarely nurtured elsewhere. But the natural piety of women was linked with an assumption of weakness and inconstancy that was to have longstanding echoes in the rhetoric of female spirituality.

By the end of the seventeenth century, this cluster of ideas about feminine spirituality had crystallized in a sense that religious conscience and internal piety were typically female. Their more violent outward manifestations were to be discouraged; the internalization of spirituality could enhance obedience and hence, orderly family life. In private first-person writing, like that of Alice Thornton, literate women explored the frustrations of marriage, economic conflicts and illness through a spiritual framework of deliverances and tests. If spirituality could promise a world of freer gender, its practical manifestations towards the end of the period were often associated with a deepening of gender divisions.

# 2   Patriarchal Households

In theory, the household was the fundamental unit of early modern society: the heart of economic, social and gender order. In a patriarchal political system, the concepts of house, household and family carried considerable ideological weight. Every government imagined itself as ruling a nation made up of households whose order mirrored that of the state, with a father implicitly bound to protect a wife, children and servants. Obedient subjects, or families, made for peace and order. The normative ideals of femininity, and even more so those of masculinity, were premised on the patriarchal household.

The concept of patriarchy has been central to feminist criticism; it was also pivotal for early modern political theorists. For historians interested in the structures which validate and maintain gender relations, patriarchy is an invaluable analytic tool. It describes a structural system in which men dominate women through labour relations, political power, male violence, sexuality and culture. It provides a critical take on social structures and cultural practices that are all too readily naturalized, partly because so many of them remain deeply familiar.

Early modern people lived not just in a general patriarchy, but a specific one which theorized the household as a microcosm of the state. Patriarchalism was the dominant political theory of the sixteenth and seventeenth centuries. Perhaps its simplest articulation came in the catechism and the Homily on Matrimony [**Doc. 28**]; its fullest explication was in the political theorist Robert Filmer's *Patriarcha*. Patriarchalism presented a parallel between the household and the commonwealth, and accordingly between the father and the king. The head of the household had power over his subjects, the family, and responsibility for them, in the same way as the monarch had over his. Resistance and disobedience undid the harmony of a kingdom, and a commonwealth of orderly families was the foundation of a secure regime. The execution of Charles I naturally posed a deep challenge to this idea of order, with its implications that the obligation to obey could be removed. By the late seventeenth century, contract theory had established a different political model for obedience in the state, requiring implicit consent rather than unquestioning obedience. The impact of this for domestic politics was not clear-cut. Gender hierarchy continued to matter to politics, but for contract theorists like Locke, the order of

DOI: 10.4324/9781003090786-4

the family and paternal authority was less a subject of explicit discussion, than a natural state of affairs.

## The Shape of the Household

While households were the central organizing unit of society and economy, they were also flexible and more complicated than contemporary descriptions allowed. As the cradle of gender roles, the household inculcated ambiguities, stresses and conflicts of authority as much as an idealized hierarchy.

The history of households and families has been central to that of gender relations since women and gender became historical subjects. Recent historiography has suggested new approaches and prompted a shift of focus. Deconstructing patriarchal ideals and their lack of resonance with practice has made it easier to historicize women's roles as wives and mothers, and to attend to men's as husbands and fathers. Histories of emotions, of courtship and of marital disputes have offered a more sophisticated analysis of the emotional tenor of early modern family life, demonstrating that high mortality rates and rigid ideas of order did not prevent the expression of romantic love, grief and passion. Early social historians described an early modern transition in family life. The cultural impact of the Reformation and the early stages of capitalism created the context for a shift from a collective society, with large, hierarchically organized family units, to a society of small nuclear households based on affective bonds and companionate marriage. More recent historians have seen companionship, love and hierarchy as co-existing in many early modern marriages; it has proved hard to trace a decisive shift in the emotional tenor of intimate relationships, and more recent work has focused on the economics and discourse of marriage.

The records of disputes over courtship and marriage, pursued through the church courts, have enabled historians to reconstruct some of the expectations that accompanied marriage at different levels of the social spectrum. Consent was critical, and women's marriages were not generally arranged, but made and agreed themselves, with advice and support from kin; many had lost at least one parent by the time they married in their mid-twenties. Elite women and men married earlier, but even planned marriages expected full consent. While ages of marriage and parental involvement varied, the language of love and choice was used from plebeian courtship to elite letters.

Demographic evidence fills out this picture. Reconstitutions of family structure have drawn on the registration of births, deaths and marriages mandated by Henry VIII to demonstrate some revealing trends about family life. New interpretations have challenged preconceptions about women's choices. Widows who did not remarry often had good reasons to remain single; in contrast, men remarried sooner, seemingly in need of female partners or housekeepers. Statistical analysis based on household tax records reveals high numbers of female-headed households in urban areas.

The patriarchal household was the context in which girls and boys learned their gender roles at first hand. At each stage of life, they had different models and specific parts to play. The early modern English household was typically small, two-generational and nuclear, with an average household size of between four or five people. Married couples lived with their children and one or more servants, but not their own parents. Single women sometimes lived together, or as lodgers, as well as in service. In densely populated urban areas, houses often included more than one household; in the great houses of the elite, as many as a hundred people lived together. Service was ubiquitous, a lifecycle experience for boys and girls of many social levels.

Actual houses and households were complicated, and the reality of domestic life ensured that the family–state analogy that was so central to political thinking could only ever be an ideal. The household-family was necessarily flexible and sometimes fragile. High mortality rates left widowers, widows and orphans who survived in the care of other relatives. Remarriages ran at a high level. At the same time, single women and widows were ordinary, not exceptional: at any one time at least half the adult female population was unmarried, and in the seventeenth century up to a fifth of women never married. Men were more likely to marry and to remarry, but for them too, intermittent or lifetime bachelorhood was a reality if not a desirable option.

The late marriage that was typical of northern European habits made for distinctive features. In parts of central and southeastern Europe, dowries and family support encouraged earlier marriage; in England and northern Europe more generally, marriage and the formation of an independent household happened later, supported by several years of work, training and saving. Between 1550 and 1700 the average age of first marriage for men was falling from 29 to 27; for women it remained around the age of 26 (Wrigley and Schofield, 1981: 423). Couples were generally expected to be of similar ages, with mismatched old men and young women one of the targets of mocking rituals. This whole pattern gave women considerable agency in the marriage process, though men still took the active role, and it also meant that a substantial proportion of the population did not marry at all. This was partly determined by economics, with hard times impacting on the age and frequency of marriage of the next generation. But it was also evident by the end of the seventeenth century that single life was becoming both more necessary and more possible. The late age of marriage throughout the period meant young women had a period of independence, arguably giving them unusual economic power (De Moor and Van Zanden, 2010).

One of the distinctive features of the early modern English family was the place of servants in it. Contractual bonds and domestic arrangements were more significant than blood ties in this respect. When diarists spoke of 'family', they meant the household members who shared living arrangements, especially servants and apprentices. Siblings living together, or bachelors or spinsters with servants, were families too. Ralph Josselin, an Essex clergyman, described the departure of his servant as 'the first to be married out of my family'; he replaced her with his sister [**Doc. 20**]. Family units were necessarily flexible, as servants and relatives came and went. Children grew up with powerful ties to temporary members of their households and role models who passed through. The relations between older children and servants could be close; often they shared beds.

Wider kinship ties were powerful in a different way. The range of kin recognized in wills has been shown to be narrow, but evidence suggests that in other circumstances, kin carried more weight. High mortality and frequent remarriage also extended the range of kin, from siblings and uncles or aunts to step-relations. High levels of mobility and migration meant that families were often isolated from relatives in their parish but maintained connections within regional communities or at a longer distance. The single and childless were likely to leave bequests to more distant kin; single women especially often left money to nieces or younger female relations. The time of service, apprenticeship and marriage was when kinship ties were called into play. Distant family members helped find places, housing and partners for young women and men leaving home. Kinship, it seems, was not so much an obligation as a resource, and it retained emotional significance. The effect of this for gender relations was somewhat liberating, compared with other patriarchal systems. The mores of behaviour were unlikely to be enforced by a large or omnipresent group of observant older kin; indeed, as young men and women became adults, they were most likely to be away from their blood relations as well as their kin. This might have allowed some freedom to build an individual identity. Similarly, most young married couples started their lives together in the context of a local neighbourhood, rather than under the eye of parents or in-laws; gender relations in adulthood must have been essentially peer-regulated, and married women were unlikely to be caring for elderly parents as well as their own children. In relation to the formation of marriage, kinship connections seem to have been used not so much to find partners, as to provide financial investment in a new union: this was the meaning of 'friend' in the context of marriage. At the same time, the relative looseness of kinship structures may well have left women in a vulnerable position. Young women migrating to London were well known to be at risk of prostitution and illegitimate pregnancy.

## The Nature of Marriage

Most sixteenth- and seventeenth-century opinion took marriage to be the lynchpin of a stable, successful life. For both women and men, adulthood was expected to involve establishing a household and probably raising children. For middling-status men, marriage often marked a transition into self-sufficiency; marriage was virtually necessary to run a business or a smallholding. For women, marriage was additionally marked by admission into different social circles and appropriate clothes. In church, a married woman typically sat in a pew instead of standing with the single people. She was invited to attend births and participated in the shared sexual knowledge of matrons. At the same time, her legal status changed radically, making her identity subject to her husband's.

In the mid-sixteenth century the Protestant Reformation launched a reforming effort at the nature and understanding of marriage, rejecting the medieval monastic idealization of celibacy in favour of a practical, human approach which stressed marriage as another route to salvation, and ultimately helped develop the idea of marriage as a contractual union, both secular and spiritual, of two loving partners. In the direst circumstances, it might be dissolved by adultery or as a result of extreme cruelty. The English Reformation did not result in a reform of marriage law as substantive as that of continental Protestant states, but it did change the context of marriage. By the end of the sixteenth century the betrothal ceremonies which had survived from medieval practice were falling out of use. The rules on annulment and separation, however, remained largely unchanged.

One of the legacies of the Reformation's response to marriage was a great deal of printed advice. John Dod and Robert Cleaver's exhaustive *A Godly Form of Household Government* treated in turn the respective duties of husbands and wives, parents and children, and masters, mistresses and servants [**Doc. 27**]. Many such texts were written by Protestant and later Puritan ministers, newly eligible to marry themselves, and experts on conjugal life; their advice not only exhorted women to obey, but tried to teach husbands how to become masters in their houses. Similar instructions reached a much wider audience through wedding sermons and homilies preached at church services; the Homily on Matrimony provided by the Elizabethan church for its clergy to preach gave a long discussion of the graces and dangers of marriage, including a firm proscription of male violence as well as prescriptions for female obedience, and noted the 'grief and pains' marriage brought for women [**Doc. 28**]. Occasionally, women wrote advice too; Dorothy Leigh's *Mother's Blessing*, reprinted frequently in the first half of the seventeenth century, took the form of a mother advising her sons [**Doc. 29**]. Almost none of this advice was new, being largely a commentary on key biblical texts, particularly Proverbs and the Pauline epistles. What was innovative was the detailed exposition of that advice in printed books and its frequent recapitulation in the pulpit. Sixteenth- and seventeenth-century women and men read and heard a set of hierarchical domestic principles that were readily invoked to castigate and discipline, and which laid out marriage as both a contract of authority and submission, and a human relationship in which power and intimacy were negotiated.

Hierarchies of gender were thus embedded in families and communities, making it hard to think outside them. The feminist texts of the late sixteenth century generally argued not for equality, but for the respective virtues of women versus men; their arguments drew on extremes to argue that either men, or women, were better. Among all the radicals of the 1650s, few went so far as to suggest women should stand side by side with men as equal citizens. The analogy of the household as state provided everyone with a clear and comprehensible model of the contractual relations of obedience, and the relationship between husband and wife provided the model of female subordination to male authority.

At the same time, the ideals of prescriptive literature were themselves contradictory, unrealistic and sometimes extreme. The logic of authority allowed for violence as a means of discipline, but the Homily on Matrimony was not unusual in treating it as unacceptable [**Doc. 28**]. Ballads and other popular literature made the enforcement and inversion of domestic hierarchy into a raucous joke, targeting particularly cuckolds who were cheated by their wives (Figure 2.1). In the preface of William Gouge's *Domesticall Duties*, he recalled his congregation complaining about his advice on the subjection of women and their lack of economic autonomy: they were not prepared to follow the letter of the law (Gouge, 1622). Clearly, these could be matters of contention, and to read household advice as either realistic description or aspirational prescription is too simplistic. The balance of power between husband and wife, and the relationship between love and domination, was worked out in the pulpit, on the printing presses and in married life.

Early modern marriage was shaped by a set of legal rules, some of which were under pressure from religious and political changes and by demographic realities. The ceremony of matrimony was a process rather than a single event, often involving months if not years of courtship, an informal betrothal and sometimes a formal contract before the ceremony in church. The potential complications of this process meant that late sixteenth-century church courts were still dealing with disputed marriage contracts. A properly made contract could, in theory, undercut a later church marriage, and one of the options for women and men whose courtships had gone awry was to pursue the other partner through the church courts. Such cases were infrequent but are rich with

*Figure 2.1* 'The Cuckold's Complaint', Pepys Ballad Collection, IV.132.
© The Pepys Library, Magdalene College, Cambridge

detail about the expectations of the courtship period. The key elements for a binding contract were witnesses; the exchange of gifts, such as gloves, bowed coins or rings; and the exchange of words taken directly from the marriage service. To offer any of these things made the tentative gestures of early courtship more formal. There were, though, plenty of ways to sidestep the final binding step of formal contracts. Promises in the future tense, or conditional ones, kept options part-way open. Sex continued to be the one binding event that made a conditional contract firm.

The rituals of courtship allocated highly gendered roles to men and women. If marriage was the time that future identity was settled, courtship was a time when women exercised a freedom to decide. They did not ask, but they responded and negotiated. Their options were still open. The rules of betrothal, which still had weight in canon law, enabled women to give men a conditional answer which they could later retract: 'if my friends agree' seems to have been a common response to a proposal, and as matters became more serious, the chaperonage of older family and friends was called for. The acceptance of rings and other gifts could be a key piece of evidence that a woman had accepted a proposal, so that for women especially, gift exchange could be compromising. The conventions of contracting left both parties room for manoeuvre, but the flexibility of informal contracts could go disastrously wrong.

While elite parents still generally assisted in arranging their children's marriages, choice was considered critical, and most women and men conducted their courtships in relative independence. Many were living away from home, in service or as apprentices, and by the time they married many had lost one or both parents. The influences on courtship were more likely to be contemporaries and employers. Those parents who were still alive were likely to be instrumental in helping to set up a first household, alongside the friends who might contribute to a woman's marriage portion, or help a man along in his trade or profession. Friends in marriage safeguarded the marital process from being driven by impulse or lust. The role of parents and friends was also a useful protection at a time of great importance. The process of betrothal and marriage exemplified the depth of kinship and friendship ties for both women and men. Remarrying widows and widowers were equally dependent on their friends, with inheritances and children to take into account.

The day-to-day relations between husbands and wives are some of the hardest historical experiences to recover. Even those who left personal writings were unlikely to write of the ordinary life of a marriage. Letters, by their nature, were written in unusual periods of absence, and while family letters can be wonderfully intimate, few collections include letters from both husbands and wives. Among those elite women who left letters, the obedience required of them was sometimes a matter for jest: Maria Thynne's letters tease out the contradictions of loving marriage, and read interestingly against her mother-in-law's more conventional ones [**Doc. 30**]. The Thynne marriage, though, was a clandestine one, much opposed by her husband's parents, and their union left a lasting bitterness between the elder Thynnes and their daughter-in-law. Neither among elites, nor among plebeians, do historians now discern a measurable shift from one type of marriage to another. The rhetoric of companionate marriage certainly became more powerful from the late seventeenth century, and is nicely reflected in the family portraits of the seventeenth and eighteenth centuries; transitions in the emotional landscape are much harder to see. Most powerful in determining the nature of marriage may be the fact that for the majority of the population, marriage was expected to be made by choice, at a relatively mature age, and with little parental pressure, but with a solid economic basis. By one calculation, at least one sixth of brides were pregnant at marriage, indicating that the ceremony could function as an affirmation of an existing relationship.

Early modern marriages were not expected to end in any way other than death. Divorce that allowed remarriage was, in law, practically impossible. Legal separations allowing couples to live apart on grounds of adultery or extreme violence, did not allow remarriage and were rare: even the large diocese of London and Middlesex dealt with fewer than ten cases a year. There were, nonetheless, ways that marriages could be ended, informally or formally. Informal separations were possible for those with the resources to support multiple households. Many elite couples – perhaps a third – lived habitually or frequently apart. Elizabeth Freke, one of several female diarists whose writings survive, was one of them [Doc. 31]. Her writing was at least partly propelled by marital disputes over property and debt. Other unhappy couples were constrained by the canon law's requirement to live together, and some were presented to the church courts for living apart without permission. There is evidence that some others simply paid the fine and remarried after a separation. Marriages could be annulled (allowing remarriage) on grounds of physical incapacity: impotence, but not infertility. The female partner of a man alleged to be impotent might be required to prove herself a virgin. Until 1563, a large number of degrees of kin could be judged prohibited, and marriages annulled, but by the later 16$^{th}$ century this was much rarer. Bigamy was more common, often semi-accidental: couples had separated, lost touch or gone abroad, and presumed or hoped that their former partner was dead [Doc. 41]. The potential for losing touch was more likely to work in favour of men than women: a woman with children was unlikely to be able to support herself alone.

While contemporaries condemned it, the law tolerated marital violence within certain limits. A woman whose husband broke those limits could bind him over to keep the peace, or sue at the church courts for separation. Only a few did. Women who sued for separation at the church courts were required to prove that the violence had been so severe they were in danger of death; accordingly, the evidence records extreme and brutal violence. Printed literature openly discussed the legitimacy of marital violence. Most agreed that, if legal, it was highly undesirable, and that a good husband should be able to persuade his wife to obey without force. In this lies a crucial difference between modern and early modern perceptions of male violence. In the seventeenth century, men's violence to their wives was often seen as a manifestation of a greater issue of subordination, and might relate to conflicts about property, children and social life [**Doc. 32**]. The image of 'A New Year's Gift for Shrews' (Figure 2.2) relates a narrative of a woman who would not be 'good' and was beaten. The violence that, exceptionally, reached the courts illuminates both where the lines of unacceptability were drawn, and the justifications that could be produced by violent men.

In the eighteenth century, a sea change in cultural representations of violence became apparent. It was no longer much discussed in public discourse; the decline in acceptability of violence generally also meant the disappearance of domestic violence from the cultural radar, though levels are still impossible to ascertain. Neighbourhood interest in marital violence could be protective, as well as dangerous for women.

*Figure 2.2 A New Yeare's Gift for Shrews.* A popular story, depicting a wife who 'will not be good' beaten by her husband and eventually sent to the devil. Print, 1625–40, 18.9 × 20.6 cm.

Neighbourly intervention in marital relations testified to the public nature of marriage. With the bond between husband and wife was at the heart of the economic household. Orderly marriages were integral to that constant concern of early modern communities, keeping the peace. Partly this was due to factors of space and architecture: it was hard to ignore what happened between husband and wife, even within the walls of the household. It was also an economic issue: the marital bond kept households economically stable. Political ideas pushed the message home: marital relations were a community concern.

Far more often than any kind of separation, early modern couples were separated by death, and at an early age. Marriage was of necessity a serial institution; as many as one in three of all marriages were second unions for at least one party. This meant that remarriage was a live issue for most families. Some men's wills even made specific reference to their wives' potential future husbands, advising them to choose well. At the same time, the cultural weight laid on women's chastity meant that the remarriage of widows could arouse tensions, manifested in often misogynist ballads, plays and jokes. The rates at which widows remarried depended partly on their financial and landholding situation. Traditional demographic arguments assume that all widows wanted or needed to remarry: in fact, a more complex reasoning came into play. Both economic evidence and personal writings reveal widows making careful decisions about how to preserve their inheritances in the light of custom and land tenure. Some rural widows inherited freebench, a right which entitled them to their husband's manorial land for life; they were more likely to remarry than those living in manors which limited a widow's inheritance if she remarried.

## Parenthood

In theory, fatherhood was the essence of patriarchy: the domestic authority of men was the bulwark of national order. Motherhood, less charged with the rhetoric of authority, had its own political associations with protection, peace and nurture of the generations necessary to the nation's future. Dorothy Leigh's widely read domestic advice articulated maternal nurture as a rationale for writing and publishing, exploring the experience of breastfeeding with a vision, reflective of contemporary humoral thinking, in which her heart's blood rushed to nourish the child at her breast [Doc. 29]. The model of the nursing mother was resonant enough to be cited not just by tracts advocating breastfeeding, but by male prophets, clergymen and monarchs describing their own role: the biblical image of the 'nursing father' united paternal authority and maternal care. The widespread practice of using wet-nurses distributed the labour of nourishing and nursing an infant far beyond the biological mother, and the choice of wet-nurse or the decision not to breastfeed was a target for moralizing advice. Towards the eighteenth century, attitudes to breastfeeding shifted, depicting it as a natural ideal of motherhood and eliding its economic value and labour (Shepard, 2017).

The demographic and economic realities of domestic life made the practice of parenthood socially variable. Elite families, who bore children earlier, maintained ties of dependence across generations and into the adult lives of children; newly married elite couples, often still in their teens, might start their lives together in the parental home. Poorer parents were less likely to maintain a grip of authority on children who left home in their teens and married later and more independently. The poorest were at risk of seeing their families absorbed and dispersed by the parish authority of 'civic fathers', who were authorized to bind out the children of the poor to parish work. By this man-oeuvre, poor parents could be dispossessed of the authority of paternity that defined elite governors. More benignly, Joan Vokins's letter home [**Doc. 33**] suggests the extended network of mothering and caring that might stand in for absent or working biological mothers.

The nature of work and domestic space meant that children in ordinary house-holds spent much time at close quarters with their parents; while the responsibility for childcare seems to have been universally female, children worked from a young age, and children's presence was a part of street life. Among elite families, there was some sense of fathers taking a greater role than mothers for their sons after breeching. Critically, though, families at all social ranks had other adults and older children sharing the care of children, and many had domestic servants who took an important role in caregiving. The concerns regularly aired by commentators on the importance of mothers breastfeeding their own children did not prevent the common use of wet-nurses, particularly for urban women.

Marriage and parenthood divided early modern women: maternity opened a world of sociability, expertise and secrets exchanged between gossips and around the rituals of childbirth. Paternal identity was less secure and less col-lective. Blood ties, the metaphor for relatedness, mattered, but paternity was necessarily putative, with no proof. Medical theories about conception and the power of maternal imagination and jokes about misidentified fathers added another layer of potential uncertainty, making discourse about paternity a potential source of anxiety in the edifice of masculinity.

## Spaces and Things

The material world of gender gives historians an insight into both concrete and abstract aspects of gender relations. Contemporary ideologies of marriage and household had a strong spatial dimension. The conceptual distinction between public and private spheres came into play towards the end of our period, but earlier on the distinction between outside and inside provided a touchstone for gender rules. The walls of the house were imagined to safeguard the house-hold's honour and the wife's honesty. The role of the husband comprised work outdoors, provisioning and labouring; that of the housewife was said to revolve around keeping and caretaking [**Doc. 27**]. Puritan marriage manuals laid stress on the dangers of vanity and display, the household keeping the wife both symbolically and practically under her husband's governance. However, while prescriptions for the gender division between outdoors and indoors were rhet-orically powerful, they did not describe actual spatial practices. Every image of early modern marketplaces featured women, both selling and buying, and a host of testimonies record women, both housewives and servants, going in and out of houses and up and down streets as a central part of their daily business. Street sellers were often women. While occasional high-handed proscriptions, such as after the May Day riots of 1517, warned men to keep their wives indoors, street life seems to have been very mixed. The enclosure of women from public space was a rhetoric rather than a practice.

Uses of domestic space gave houses a history of their own, one that differentiated space by gender and by age and status. The study of household space has mostly been at the level of the great houses. There, the great shift in building styles meant a transition from houses with great halls where much of daily life was lived, towards more differentiated spaces like upstairs bedchambers and separate kitchens, where husbands and wives, children and servants lived and worked separately. In the great houses, by the seventeenth century the growing trend for closets for reading had already given elite men and women another kind of space to themselves.

In most houses, gender segregation was minimal. Despite the sermons and advice-writers' repetition of biblical advice that women should keep to the house and men to the outside world, actual patterns of work, marketing and housewifery made this unlikely to happen. The number of slanderous exchanges between women that took place on doorsteps, though, suggests that the house's threshold held a symbolic and practical significance. Within most houses, the closely-connected rooms ensured that women and men of all ages spent most of their time in a heterosocial world. Birthing rooms were exceptional in creating an exclusively female space, though they may not have been as sealed and separate as ritual prescribed.

The marriage bed, usually the most expensive piece of furniture in the house, and hung with draperies for warmth and privacy, underlined and symbolized the bodily unity of husband and wife. In a marital dispute in seventeenth-century London, Anne Young resorted to her own room after a violent dispute with her husband; forsaking his bed was symbolic of their relationship breakdown and was cited by her husband as key evidence against her when she sued for a separation [**Doc. 32**].

The history of material objects adds an important dimension to that of gender. As material goods and their ownership diversified in the seventeenth century, retail shopping became part of gendered leisure patterns, as well as women's labour both as shopkeepers and shoppers. More specialized and fashionable objects acquired gendered meanings: cooking utensils, embroideries, and books carried emotional and economic weight and symbolic messages. New foods and drinks were imbued with codes of gender and colonialism. Drinking coffee in coffee-houses was typically represented as a masculine pastime, involving civic discourse and public news; in housewives' guides, Kim Hall has argued, the colonial trade in sugar was domesticated through women's work making conserves and confectionery (Hall, 1996).

## Divisions of Labour

The household was also, most essentially, an economy, in which labour relations were organized around the relations of husband, wife, servant and apprentice. Contemporary religious prescriptions identified husbands as workers and earners, wives as keepers and spenders. Actual practice for working families was quite different, and dependent on a different model of gendered labour: more overlapping, though still restrictive and hierarchical. Housewifery loomed large in advice literature, with texts like Gervase Markham's *The English Housewife* (1615) setting out a model for women's work growing vegetables, making medicines, dairy work, preserving and making clothes. Much of this work was shared between mistresses and servants, although cooking was becoming central to servants' work, and larger households were employing separate cooks or cookmaids.

Married women's work was far from entirely domestic, nor was it necessarily tied to that of their husbands. In practice the marital economy often depended on men's and women's separate, as well as overlapping, work, and many women described themselves as maintaining themselves and as having occupations. The best evidence for the variety of roles women undertook comes, so far, from urban sources. In the court records of late seventeenth-century London, a majority of married women described separate occupations, including sewing, knitting, cleaning and washing, market selling, victualling and nursing (Erickson, 2008). Some such work was domestic, some peripatetic; urban wives and daughters also contributed to the trades and crafts operated in their husbands' names. Where guilds, the strongholds of masculine artisanal identity, regulated labour, female participation was a subject of contest, but widows habitually took over their husbands' trades, notably in printing, and girls could also be apprenticed, typically though not exclusively as seamstresses and into housewifery. Married women's legal restrictions in trade could be circumvented by the custom of many boroughs to allow them **feme sole** trader status, which enabled them to trade as if single and protected their husbands from their debts.

The horizons of single women's work changed over the period. Sixteenth and early seventeenth century urban authorities sometimes tried to rule against women 'working at their own hands', invoking the laws that regulated labour to compel them into service or other employment under a household head. In the second half of the seventeenth century, improved economic conditions and a widening market sector opened up space for single women to trade, particularly in making and selling clothes and food.

Divisions of labour varied across the country and by occupational sector. Craft work, mostly in towns, was sharply divided by gender. Agricultural work involved more overlap between male and female tasks, and a more flexible division of labour. Commercial roles were less rigid than contemporary literature suggested, with both sexes heavily involved in buying and selling, but women dominated in the sale of textiles. The relationship between women's work and the house was far from synonymous. While housework and care work might have accounted for a third of women's working hours, it was not their only or their dominant task. As well, many of the tasks of housewifery, like doing laundry and fetching water, were done outside. Many houses were also workshops in which crafts and shops were based. The large service sector meant that unpaid housework and care work was less important in women's work lives than we might expect.

Prestigious occupations and guilds made a habit of excluding women's work. Tailors defended themselves everywhere against the incursions of seamstresses, but during the seventeenth century the move towards looser, less tailored garments like the mantua and the spread of ready-made clothes and accessories gave women many ways to make a living from sewing. Nursing, washing and cleaning was persistently a female sector, providing often poorly paid employment for women. New technologies typically changed the status and the gender balance of occupations. Brewing provides a good example. Traditionally a largely domestic process, the occupational term 'brewster', with a 'st' like spinster and huckster, demonstrated its association with women, but by the seventeenth century it was a largely male occupation, and women's participation had been marginalized. A combination of factors was responsible. Supervision of brewing increased, and men rather than women were licensed, often employing their wives. Ale began to be eclipsed by beer as the staple drink; the addition of hops meant more beer could be produced from one brewing, and economies of scale became evident. The need for more space and more credit to facilitate larger, less frequent brewings took beer out of the household economy, and particularly out of the reach of single women. At the same time, the older image of the alewife as a good housewife was replaced by anxieties about alewives as dishonest corrupters of both men and drink (Bennett, 1996). Midwifery, a distinctively female occupation at the beginning of the period, was a special case, supported by informal training and regulated by oaths before the bishop. It drew on an essentialized, corporeal expertise which was generally taken to be unique to women; Jane Sharp's *Midwives' Book* had much to say about the special practical knowledge of women delivering other women. Even there, though, published guides to childbirth cast shade on women's competence, and the initially mysterious technology of forceps was kept a trade secret by the men who introduced them.

Gender roles and relations play an increasingly important part in the historiography of economic change: the history of work demands attention to women's labour both in and out of the family, to the impact of changes in labour relations on gender relations, and to the effect of ideas about gender on work practices. Throughout the period, the work that men did was recorded more fully and formally than that of women. Men claimed occupational identities to which women rarely had access. The nursing, cleaning, washing, and most of all the caring that women did in houses, whether their own or those of others, is often invisible. In recent research, historians have used legal records to track the gendered use of time rather than named occupations, and these findings demonstrate both the gendering of different work tasks, and the amount of labour that women put into the economy. The low pay and lack of occupational categories of working women did not reflect the significance of their labour.

The impact of commercial expansion and capitalist development on women's work has been much debated. Starting with the work of Alice Clark in 1919, some historians have seen women's work becoming devalued and marginalized in the late seventeenth century as the household economy of complementary roles was replaced by sharply divided male and female work for the market (Clark, 1992). Certainly, the long-term transition to wage labour devalued women's domestic work, though the self-subsistent household was already characterized by hierarchical conceptions of gendered labour. Equally striking to recent historians have been the continuities in the relative positions of women's and men's work through the medieval and early modern periods, and indeed into the modern. Women's wages were consistently half to two-thirds that of men's; they laboured in the sectors of service, domestic work, food provision and cleaning, the same areas in which low-paid women's work is clustered today (Erickson, 1992). Jan de Vries's model of an 'industrious revolution' that preceded the industrious revolution adds another dimension to the narrative of change, arguing that this expansion of production was underpinned by women's work in spinning, knitting and sewing. The demand for new consumer goods from 1650 substantially increased married women's work for the market, and also brought greater autonomy (De Vries, 1994). The high numbers of single women in early modern England also mean that the marital household cannot be the sole measure of women's economic contribution. The diversification of urban work, with shops and schools, offered new opportunities for enterprising women with some resources in the late seventeenth century.

The persistent continuities in the low status, limited opportunities, and poor reward of women's work over the period support Judith Bennett's model of 'patriarchal equilibrium', in which male privilege adapts easily to changing circumstances, perpetuating female disadvantage (Bennett, 2006). But recent research stresses the importance of valuing the time women spent on work and the initiative and industry that made them active participants in economic change (Shepard, 2015).

The ease with which most men named themselves, in official circumstances, by occupation suggests a relationship between work and identity that was much more straightforward than it could be for women, and historically, men's occupations have been seen as fundamental to their identities. In practice, the occupations recorded for many men were only partially accurate; like women, particularly in urban areas, their working lives might involve a portfolio of roles. The economic crises of the late sixteenth century also complicated male occupational security. With rapidly rising population and high inflation, underemployment was becoming a widespread problem. In many urban areas the transition through the stages of work from apprentice, through journeyman, to master was becoming harder for men to achieve. Journeymen were shut out from the opportunity to become masters, and ended up as permanent wage labourers, a position of little earning power and low repute. Agricultural labourers found it harder to establish their own smallholdings. A significant proportion of men could not muster the economic resources to marry and support a household. Their position in communities, short of all the evidence of functional manhood, could be problematic. As men but not masters, they were excluded from what has been called the 'patriarchal dividend', the advantages that the patriarchal system offered to men as a group (Connell, 2009: 142). Alehouse culture, gambling, violence and 'ill rule' provided an alternative means of self-assertion to the respectability of the successful householder. The fragility of economic autonomy was instrumental in producing the hierarchies of masculinity that characterized early modern gender relations.

## Economic Roles

Through the early modern period and into the modern era, the economic dimension of gender defined women by their marital status, treating wives as largely economically incompetent. Early modern women's relationship with property was complex, varying with legal jurisdictions, types of property, age and marital status, but marriage was by far the major factor compromising their economic identity and capacity. The rules of coverture, the common law doctrine that subsumed a woman's legal identity into her husband's, were peculiarly strict in England. A wife could hold neither real (land) nor personal property (moveable goods) in her own right [**Doc. 34**]. Other jurisdictions, including equity, chancery and borough custom, offered some redress, and both propertied women and their families used legal means to protect their goods and their children's inheritances. Over the period, though, the dominance of common law was growing and traditional rights such as widows' entitlement to a third of their husbands' moveable property were legislated away.

One side-effect of these constraints was a flourishing variety of financial instruments to allow women to hold some goods in their own names. Women with money and their families used bonds, settlements, contracts and trusts to evade the implications of coverture, revealing a significant degree of financial and legal awareness. Elizabeth Freke navigated her way around the financial constraints of marriage with the help of her father, who was clear-eyed about the risks of her husband having complete financial autonomy [**Doc. 31**]. Anne Clifford spent years fighting to inherit her family's estates; one of the eventual outcomes when she did so was the monumental 'great picture' which she commissioned to narrate her struggle and set her in the framework of her ancestors (Figure 2.3). Like other landed women in the period, her connection to the estates to which she was born was imperilled by her sex. Moveable goods and money, the main resources of those without land, were harder to control. In practice, married women bought, sold and kept goods without reference to the law, but its constraints were well known, and the framework of marital dependency also impacted on women's more general capacity to hold authority.

While married women were particularly economically disadvantaged by English law, single women were comparatively free. Elsewhere in Europe single women often needed guardians to engage in contracts and economic

*Figure 2.3 The Great Picture* by Jan van Belcamp (1610–53) (attr.). Commissioned by Lady Anne Clifford in 1646, when she attained her inheritance, the centre panel depicts her parents, the Countess and Earl of Cumberland, and brothers before her birth; the side panels show herself in youth and age. The portraits on the wall show her family and her tutor and governess. Oil on canvas, 1646. Centre panel: 254 × 254 cm; side panels: 25 × 119.38 cm.
© Abbot Hall Art Gallery/Bridgeman Images.

arrangements; in England they could operate much as men did. In the late seventeenth century, single women and widows joined the small investors who were part of the financial revolution. Their investments have been traced in the Bank of England, in the stock market and in the Virginia and East India Companies. Women were also exporters and merchants in transatlantic trading systems, owned warehouses, and provisioned ships. Studies of individual entrepreneurs have illuminated the strategies of women such as Joyce Jeffreys, a mid-seventeenth-century Hereford gentlewoman who made a career lending money from her inheritance, and Hester Pinney, a lace trader from Bristol who expanded her family's business to London, keeping a shop and managing investments (Spicksley, 2012; Sharpe, 1999). Evidence of women's investments suggests a widely varying set of approaches, not necessarily typified by the caution that is often attributed to women's financial management (Froide, 2016).

Research into women's economic activity offers important challenges to standard narratives. Amy Erickson argues that both single women's freedom to move money, and the complex financial instruments developed for and by married women, had a significant impact on the early development of capitalism in England. The peculiar combination of restrictions and freedoms on English women's property transactions may have facilitated the flow of capital that enabled the financial revolution (Erickson, 2005). In this field, gender history continues to challenge assumptions about female agency and the impact of the law.

## Service and Apprenticeship

Lifecycle service meant that young women and men typically served out their teenage years in another household. They grew to adulthood largely away from their parents, working for low wages, supervised by a married couple and sometimes alongside other servants. In a population weighted towards the young, servants and apprentices played an important, though subordinate, role in households and communities, particularly in urban areas. Around half the households in early modern England employed servants, the majority only one. Between the ages of fourteen and their early twenties, young men were typically working as servants in husbandry or in craft and trade apprenticeships to crafts and trades, young women in domestic service, or sometimes as apprentices in housewifery or crafts. Their tasks and living situations varied, but the common features distinguished male and female servants sharply. Apprentices and male farm servants were training to become masters or husbandmen themselves: the aim was to amass enough skills to move from dependence to autonomy, the epitome of full manhood, supported by a wife. Service for women, in contrast, offered a period of comparatively more independence than the economic subordination of marriage. For both sexes, the long-term effects of the economic crisis of the late sixteenth century meant that by the early seventeenth century marriage was becoming less likely.

Biographical and autobiographical accounts shed light on the experiences of youth. Edward Barlow's story of departure depicts his mother longing to hang onto him and his father letting him go; he construes himself in the mould of a self-reliant young man whose ambitions lie far from the drudgery of agricultural labour or the uncertain rewards of apprenticeship [**Doc. 35**] (Figure 2.4). Young

*Figure 2.4* Edward Barlow leaving home, with his mother behind him. Drawing in Barlow's journal, 1695–1703. Ink on paper, 36 × 24 cm.
© National Maritime Museum, Greenwich, UK.

women's plans are less well recorded, but the potential of urban life loomed especially large for women, aware of the constraints of other opportunities; urban service almost always offered better wages than agricultural work. Once employed, servants continued to be mobile, working on flexible contracts and often hired annually. Before she ended up at London's **Bridewell**, Mawdlin Gawen followed a not unusual pattern of short-term work across two counties and with various employers, some relatives [**Doc. 10**]. Sixteenth and seventeenth-century evidence records servants of African heritage, some treated as freer than others, many described as belonging to, or 'of', their masters and mistresses. In Bristol, Dinah, 'a Black', had probably been brought to England in slavery, had found a way to work with some degree of freedom, but was then nearly forcibly transported back to a plantation by her mistress. The 'spiriting' of young poor people into indentured service was a well-known problem; Dinah's story was a different one [**Doc. 6**].

For most of those in service, adolescence was characterized both by a degree of independence from parents and a bound subordination in another household. The consequent emotional complexities could include close ties between children and servants, or conflicts between mistress and maidservants The tensions of apprenticeship were well attested to in contemporary literature. Apprentices were being trained, eventually, to become masters themselves; but in the meantime they were dependent on their employers' goodwill for everything, and subject to the orders of their mistresses, which some resented. Clothes, food and health provided perpetual sources of complaint for apprentices establishing their manhood through relations with masters, mistresses and fellow servants. Edward Barlow's reminiscences of apprenticeship in Lancashire in the mid-seventeenth century describe a marginal, resented position at the end of the household table; his fellow apprentice also suggested, to his displeasure, that the reward of service was to marry a daughter of the house [**Doc. 35**]. For young women, the risks of service included sexual harassment and, sometimes, sexual relations, rape and pregnancy. Of the illegitimacy cases that were dealt with by the courts, the majority concerned servants pregnant by masters or their friends and family: the conditions of employment put young women at risk. Service and apprenticeship also put the young in key positions in domestic disputes. Their evidence was frequently crucial to marriage separations and often to other legal cases, and the lines of loyalty within divided households might fall unpredictably.

While early modern service was intimate, familiar and unstructured, it was very much part of a hierarchy. Servants were at risk of disciplinary violence, and of sexual suspicions and vulnerabilities. Given the importance of adolescence in the development of individual gender identities, it is worth considering the impact of these domestic conditions.

## Single Life

Single life for both men and women offered some autonomy, but, particularly at the start of the period, and while relatively young, they were still expected to be under the authority of a patriarchal household. The Statute of Artificers (1563) decreed that those between 12 and 40 years old, out of service and without a certain level of property could be compelled into service; it was invoked most often against single women working 'at their own hand', who were perceived to be particularly awkward in the late sixteenth and early seventeenth centuries, when inflation and demographic expansion were making the balance of employment fragile in many places. Single women were an easy scapegoat.

By the middle of the seventeenth century, both women and men were marrying less often, and later. Of those born between 1562 and 1566, only 4 per cent remained unmarried; of those born between 1602 and 1606, the proportion was as high as 24 per cent, though this figure is probably distorted by clandestine and unofficial marriages in the mid- to late seventeenth century. Numbers of single people remained high through the later seventeenth century, falling again with the generations born in the 1680s. Of course, not marrying does not necessarily mean staying celibate: the actual relationships of the unmarried are almost entirely invisible. Living together without marriage, however, remained socially as well as spiritually unacceptable. At the least, these figures suggest that by the second half of the seventeenth century, staying single was no longer exceptional. Some of this change was forced by economic factors: marriage still meant economic independence, and it was harder for men to get to the point of being able to start their own households. By the later years of the seventeenth century, it was also becoming more feasible for women to live a single life. London's Royal Exchange was full of seamstresses running stalls in their own names. In small towns, expanding textile industries offered opportunities that enabled women to support themselves. Proto-industrialization is sometimes seen as encouraging early marriage, by enabling women to earn enough to marry earlier; but it also had the opposite effect of making self-sufficiency more possible.

The numbers of single people in society belie the picture often painted by contemporaries, of a world composed of nuclear households. Every household listing includes significant numbers of single women heading households, usually widows, often with spinster daughters or dependent children. Single women were also often prominent in the local economy. While the difficulty of making a living alone meant that single women and widows were always the majority of poor relief recipients, sometimes providing useful services in exchange for pensions and charity, at the other end of the economic spectrum probate records reveal single women lending extensively, both charitably and for business purposes. Women who could survive on their own had a reliable level of personal wealth and access to ready money. In some areas women were increasingly able to access legacies before they married; they were also likely to be bequeathed cash. Lending money to friends also, presumably, helped stabilize single women's social position in the local community, creating another kind of credit. Married women did not leave wills, due to coverture; but in one study of single women's wills, 42–45 per cent of urban single women mentioned money lent out, not only to individuals but to town corporations (Froide, 2005: 130–6).

The word spinster evolved in a way that reflected the priorities of social control. Originally descriptive of women who worked at spinning, by the early seventeenth century it was also being used to describe a woman who had not yet married; eventually, in the early eighteenth century, it came to denote a woman permanently single. A number of the female professional writers of the late seventeenth century celebrated the single life and their freedom from marriage. Simultaneously, though, the phrase 'old maid' appeared and became pejorative, with satires depicting old maids as desperate and sinister. The reality of independent single life that some women were achieving was unlikely to be reflected in the cultural landscape of late seventeenth-century England.

For men, marriage continued to mark economic competence and social normativity. It was difficult for either men or women to make a living, or run a smallholding, alone. Unlike single women, though, bachelors did not face an array of negative stereotypes, and they were less likely to be socially or legally disciplined into marriage or service. The model of manhood was not underpinned by the kinds of cultural censure that were directed at women.

# 3   Communities

Early modern women and men lived in communities that were both physically and morally dense. Often, the period 1450–1750 has been identified with a transition from a community of ethical neighbourly bonds to one of individualistic, commercialized stratification; with an integration of local communities into national ones; and with a redrawing of the bonds between person and community. More recently, historians have stressed the continuities with older habits of reciprocity: individualism did not have to run counter to community. Community structures and social relations were deeply inflected by sexual hierarchies, particularly in relation to poverty, sexual morality, rituals, religious roles and political participation. Women's role was significant and open to challenge, and gender relations were frequently perceived as a flashpoint for order.

## The Parish

Tudor government increasingly treated the parish as the crucible of social and economic relations. In both rural and urban areas, the parish church provided a space, a time and an identity, ordering not just social relations, but gender. Parish churches expected a predictable local weekly congregation, and well into the seventeenth century some places still had seating plans. The weekly arrangement of the congregation was both a familiar and regular ritual of community life and a point of contest. Seating was habitually arranged by status and by gender. After the Reformation moved from a tradition of standing, often in single-sex groups, towards fixed seating, but they preserved some traditional spatial distinctions. Those of higher social status sat nearer the chancel, traditionally the holiest point of the church building. While family pews were appearing, reflecting the importance of the family in Reformation teaching, separate men's and women's seating was also crystallizing older traditions. In some, men sat near the altar and women further back, confirming a tradition of female impurity. In others, the axis was east/west, placing men nearer the south door and women on the north side, protected from the outer world. In this position they would also be directly facing the conventional placement of the Virgin on Christ's right hand in the rood screen. Lady chapels

DOI: 10.4324/9781003090786-5

and carvings of the Virgin were usually on the same side, and seem to have been, before the Reformation, the particular responsibility of female parishioners. Not everyone had a seat: servants and single people were often expected to stand, and places for children could be a problem. The rights of people to pew space and the system of pew rents led, sometimes, to pew disputes fought out with insults, pokes and shoves. Women's prominence in these disputes suggests their role as figureheads in local hierarchies and as monitors of behaviour in church.

The relationship of men and women to the building of the church reflected different patterns of devotion and spiritual involvement. Historically, women and men had been equally likely to leave bequests to their parish church, but with a different emphasis: men were more likely to donate to the fabric of the building, women to single out certain guilds, altars or lights dedicated to saints. The changes of the long, piecemeal Protestant Reformation had a variable impact on women's place in the church. Separate seating was no longer prescribed, and baptism prayers no longer differentiated by sex; women's contributions to managing feasting and fasting were no longer needed, and the few women listed as churchwardens in the earlier sixteenth century disappeared by 1560. At the same time, a precise, household-focused gender order was reinscribed in the texts that replaced images on church walls, sometimes referring specifically to marital duties. One Northamptonshire church carried the text from Colossians 3: 'Husbands, love your wives, and be not bitter to them' (Peters, 2003: 189).

## Authority

The parish was part of a network of participatory institutions, including manors, wards and vestries, that maintained local order against a backdrop of demographic, economic and religious change, and with a growing system of bureaucracy and record-keeping. Such institutions worked through the assertion of authority: historians have placed varying degrees of stress on negotiation and participation, and on exclusion and subordination. All these practices and experiences of authority were gendered, and their development had implications for what it meant to be male and female.

The expansion of local government redefined the obligations of masculinity. Middling-status men were expected to internalize, transmit and police the values of the orderly state; with husbandmen and craftsmen joining their superiors in taking office, participation in governance was for many a defining feature of adult masculinity. This was particularly evident in administration-heavy urban parishes, and in communities where Puritan convictions of civic responsibility for reform were strong.

Formal participation in government largely excluded women. The words *respectable* and *substantial* denoted men who helped govern; they were unlikely to be used of women. Women's marginalization from the official project of governance was hardly new, but it was being articulated in sharper terms. By the late sixteenth century any flexibility in officeholding had been eliminated by the establishment of more systematic patterns of administration, including the rotation of office by households. Householding, so central a plank in the edifice of middling-sort participation, did not carry the same civic obligations for women as it did for men; female householders, of whom there were plenty, were expected to nominate a deputy to do their duties. Being female came to be an active disqualification for many of the core acts of citizenship in the early modern state.

Moreover, women's place in relation to government was also defined by their being likely to be the subjects of male authority. Patriarchal theory described a system in which wives were subject to their husbands, not necessarily one in which all women were subject to all men; but local government involved repeated instances of men exercising general authority over women. Seventeenth-century constables searched 'suspicious' women on the streets, and Bridewell dealt with a stream of female 'nightwalkers' (Miller, 2019; Griffiths, 1998). Poor law administration had an established gender dynamic: administrators, in the roles of churchwardens and overseers, were men, and most of the recipients were women. Particularly in hard times, one of the central duties of the lower ranks of officeholders was dealing with the poor: they were charged with overseeing paupers and ensuring the parish did not suffer too many claims on its funds. The dynamics of local government were thus likely to be shaped sharply along lines of gender, as substantial men disciplined poor women.

At the same time, the wives of those substantial men were involved in the governing process. Early modern conceptions of the marital unit presented husband and wife as an intertwined couple, whose credit and honour were bound together; the interdependent nature of identity must have reinforced this. Formal officeholding might be just the tip of the iceberg.

Despite all this, women were not entirely absent from the formal and less formal processes of government. Throughout the sixteenth and most of the seventeenth centuries, women played specific, significant roles in parish and community life, their authority largely confined to areas typically associated with female responsibilities. Women's expertise over reproduction, based largely on their experience as mothers, qualified them especially as midwives and matrons; sworn midwives held an official role regulated by the church courts, and were regularly called upon to testify to the parentage of illegitimate children. Women led the neighbourhood monitoring of illicit sex, illegitimacy and, more dramatically, infanticide. Their roles as concerned mistresses, mothers, servants and neighbours gave them a substantial stake in the moral community. Suspicions of illegitimate pregnancy or infanticide were pursued with gossip, observation and sometimes physical searches. Outside the domestic realm, women were engaged to act as keepers and matrons in hospitals for the poor and to supervise pauper apprenticeships. It was women, too, particularly the old and poor, who provided food to those quarantined for plague and searched the dead for signs of disease, providing the raw material for the Bills of Mortality. Perceived as risks of infection, the nominated searchers were then ordered to carry distinguishing sticks, walk by the gutter and avoid large groups [Doc. 36]. The authority for this work stemmed from the established associa-tion of women with the world of reproduction and the work of nursing and washing, as well as the authority of mistresses over their female servants.

It was 'matrons', older women who were usually married, who dominated in this world. The world of women involved competition and exclusion, targeting most obviously poor women, pregnant single women and maidservants. Good order required everyone to observe and intervene: women were at least as likely to do this as men, and their 'natural' sphere gave them a specific realm in which to do so. Gender adds another dimension to Keith Wrightson's influential argument that the governors and the governed had different concepts of order (Wrightson, 1980). Women's experience of being governed was shaped by gender as well as social status; but they also participated officially and unoffi-cially in the maintenance of order, and their association with sexual morals may have given them a particular sense of priorities in local government.

## Poverty

One of the defining features of early modern English society was the emergence of a stigmatized class of 'the poor': those who received relief rather than con-tributing to it, who were considered indigent rather than self-sufficient, and who constituted both the rationale for parish government, and a burden on it. Gender relations were central to the social dynamics of poverty

The piecemeal construction of the Elizabethan Poor Laws, through the var-ious acts of 1599–1601, made parishes responsible for enumerating and relieving their poor. Every list of pensions and ad hoc grants of money features a familiar profile in which poor widows were the most likely to need and receive support. In a society increasingly ready to discriminate between the deserving and the undeserving poor, widows often made themselves more deserving by being what parishes called 'helpful': washing and nursing the disabled or cleaning. Old and poor women were a familiar, useful feature of early modern England. Their indigence was less unsettling than that of men.

Poor women were ubiquitous in early modern society, yet very little of the literature on poverty acknowledges its utterly gendered nature. Being single without money or family support left women profoundly vulnerable, for very little work would pay a woman a living wage, especially as they grew older and lost the capacity for hard physical labour or fine sewing. The majority of poor relief recipients were women, and particularly old women and widows; the majority of those taxed were men.

Single mothers experienced the penalties of both poverty and the law espe-cially harshly. Parish officers regularly removed pregnant single women to avoid them settling there, and once delivered they could be whipped, and in the seventeenth century imprisoned, with justices assuming and ensuring they would not be able to care for a child. Some children went to a parish wetnurse, where life expectancy was often short. The ready assumption of the infanticide statute of 1624, that single women were likely to keep pregnancies secret and then kill their newborns, betrayed a conviction that single motherhood was economically and socially impossible [**Doc. 37**]. Abandonment, as elsewhere in Europe, could be seen as an act of mercy or a plea for charity. Single mothers with some means, however, were able to find ways to keep or provide for their children.

## Crime and the Law

The common law of early modern England was the harshest regulator of women's roles, defining married women as subject to their husbands, without a legal identity of their own and incapable of holding property in their own names. Yet the legal system was flexible and complex, and the common law, based on precedent and defined in the courts, was not the only jurisdiction. English law derived from a variety of sources, and was practised in a series of jurisdictions; the flexibility of the system sometimes offered women ways around male authority. The relationship of gender to law encompasses the differences between male and female criminality, and their treatment in the courts; the extent to which the law differentiated by sex; and the capacity of women and men to use the law in the service of dispute and conciliation.

Early modern law invoked gender both explicitly and implicitly. Few laws singled out women and the enforcement of male superiority came through assumptions as much as literal insistence. But inherent to the common law was an understanding of married women as subject to severe legal disabilities [**Doc. 34**]. For women, marital status mattered at law in a way it never did to men. English coverture, the treatment of married women as subject to their husbands, was perhaps the harshest in Europe. That, and the impossibility of divorce, put a legal cage around married women.

There were some ways around coverture. Alongside the common law, other jurisdictions allowed married women more manoeuvre. Canon law, used in the church courts, allowed women to prosecute their own cases, and it was there that women sued for the right to separate from their husbands. In cases of sexual defamation, they also sued other women. Equity law, practised at Chancery and in a number of other courts, tempered the severity of the common law with a more flexible approach to married women's property, enabling them to use settlements, jointures, trusts and personal property to protect land and goods at marriage and in widowhood, though this required considerable planning. The Court of Requests was a particularly accessible option for some, until its collapse in 1640. The variability of manorial law and borough custom also meant widows' rights could depend on where they lived. By the end of the period, ecclesiastical law and custom were marginalized by the common law; there were fewer places wives could sue in their own right and it was harder to protect women's inheritances.

In local communities and in households, the operation of law was responsive to community concerns. The 'common peace', a notion central to English law, had gendered implications. Keeping order might mean preventing women from scolding, or men from beating their wives. Disruptions to gender roles and unruly women were emblematic of disorder, and of concern to Puritan governors and village crowds alike. Early modern laws reached deep into everyday life, and past the modern boundary of privacy. Heresy and conscience, sedition, sexual offences, marital harmony and working on the Sabbath all came within the remit of the law. Most of these offences of social and moral order impacted on gender relations, with women and men both instigating prosecutions and being prosecuted. Canon law regulated sex and marriage, and hence the relationship of heterosexual partnerships to the community and the state. The pace and extent of prosecution of social and moral offences was key in setting the stage of gender relations. Two factors emerge as especially significant in determining the prosecution of moral and social offences: economic difficulties and religious tensions.

The role of the state and its governing elites in enforcing the law was always limited by the readiness of people to prosecute. Crimes and civil offences needed people to observe, inform and prosecute. Criminal prosecution was unlikely, therefore, to follow an elite agenda; it demanded if not consensus, then collaboration. The increasing stress on middling sort men's role in governing meant that administering justice was, for some men, part of their identity, drawing on the values of respectability, loyalty and religion. Puritan values stressed active citizenship and made governance the respectable man's duty. Law was not an entirely masculine endeavour. While judges, juries and magistrates had to be men, women might be called to sit on the 'jury of matrons', whose deliberations determined whether convicted felons were found pregnant, and hence temporarily saved from the gallows. Informally, women sometimes searched the bodies of other women when infanticide or illegitimacy was suspected. Women were also quite ready to mobilize the law's resources. Recognizances, a way of binding over petty offenders to keep the peace, were a particularly useful resource for women. Women regularly acted as important witnesses, with special expertise in trials for infanticide and witchcraft, and their testimony can be seen as involving significant agency; but it was also easy to discredit their words in court with allegations of financial dependence, poverty or sexual dishonour.

The sixteenth century saw a huge expansion in litigation. Across the variety of civil and ecclesiastical courts, men and women from a wide range of social statuses brought legal action over debt, trespass, property, slander and other complaints. At **Chancery**, at the church courts and at the Elizabethan **Court of Requests**, married women both sued and were sued, their sphere of action surpassing by far the restricted roles laid on them by common law; elsewhere, single women sued independently, and married women often acted as joint litigants with their husbands. Law became an important tool in the negotiation of family and local relationships.

While men were generally the majority of convicted criminals, the figures sometimes conceal female participation, such as in collaborative thefts, and women also took a part in detecting crime. Most homicides and violent assaults were committed by men against men, though women were not immune from fighting or brutalizing servants and apprentices. The murder of a husband by his wife was so heinous a reversal of order that it was deemed petty treason, and punished with burning, like heresy. A flourishing genre of cheap print and drama publicized such tales, which were in reality extremely rare; the fictions, at least, suggested both the monstrosity of female murderers and the dilemma of women brutalized by their husbands or forced into unhappy marriages. In practice, women were much more likely to be killed by their husbands than the other way round.

Violence was entrenched in the exercise of state power, and to a more debatable extent, in domestic patriarchy; it was a problematic aspect of masculinity, at once functional and disruptive. Arguably, violence against servants, children and wives lay on a spectrum of enforced power that was also manifested in public whippings and brandings. Appropriate discipline, enforced by the threat of violence, was a feature of male authority, while models of masculinity urged moderation to balance it. In social conflicts between men, violence expressed competition and status. A fight was a reasonable response to an insult, and cuffs, boxes on the ears and slaps on the face could be used to restore honour [Doc. 38]. By the end of the seventeenth century, though, public violence between men was appearing significantly less frequently in the legal records, suggesting the dissemination of new norms of male conflict and authority: it was replaced in part by public insult.

A few crimes were distinctively female. Infanticide usually involved single women being prosecuted for the death of their newborn children, and was defined by a new law in 1624, which effectively presumed the guilt of those who hid their pregnancies. As with many capital offences, judges were reluctant to convict. Witchcraft was largely a female crime and, less dramatically, so was scolding, an offence of disorderly speech. Buying stools to duck scolds was one of the ways sixteenth-century parishes demonstrated their commitment to order. At the end of the seventeenth century a different kind of gendered crime registered economic shifts: a new statute in 1699 making shoplifting a capital offence was aimed at female thieves, who made up half of those accused at the Old Bailey.

Illicit sex and illegitimate pregnancy led most often to the punishment of women. While the law penalized both partners or parents, mothers generally ended up bearing the brunt of it, only partly because they were easier to track down. Imprisonment of men who had fathered illegitimate children was avoided because of their economic responsibility, and when in 1593 Parliament considered having them whipped, members were concerned at the prospect of gentlemen being whipped at, as they said, the word of a whore. Rape, in contrast, was a serious, capital offence invariably involving men. Its very seriousness meant that prosecutions were infrequent and unlikely to lead to successful conviction.

The most famously gendered crime was witchcraft. Belief in witchcraft and a conviction that witches were mostly female were both embedded in early modern English culture. The ideas in play drew on both ancient and contemporary misogyny; the mysteries of the reproductive body; the power of magic to explain agricultural crises, hard times and everyday accidents; and the domestic and community roles of women. The English witchcraft trials combined traditional beliefs about maleficent magic with ideas about demonic pacts and sabbath meetings that were current in contemporary European literature. While successive radical feminist interpretations have presented witches as victims of a transhistorical regime of male domination, scholars of English witchcraft (many of whom would also identify as feminist) have looked at the precise configurations of prosecutions to present a more complicated picture. Misogyny was embedded in many other dynamics.

While English witchcraft trials were part of a European and Scandinavian wave, they were characterized by relative constraint. Only the trials orchestrated by **Matthew Hopkins** in the mid-seventeenth century bore much resemblance to the large-scale witch 'crazes' that featured in places such as Germany. English witches were hanged, not burned, and they were not tortured for confessions, though the Hopkins trials made use of sleep deprivation, and the power dynamics between accused witches, mostly poor, and elite male magistrates had a significant impact on the confessions. Their records, in both popular pamphlets and court documents, offer a rich insight into dangerous beliefs and everyday power dynamics. Witches were tempted by animal familiars or by the Devil himself, in relationships that had aspects of the maternal or the sexual. They damaged food, drink, children and small animals, all in the arena of women's work. The classic explanation of early modern English witchcraft, which stressed anxiety about poverty in the light of the post-Reformation reconfiguration of charity, highlighted the dynamics of needy, poor women on the margins of cohesive neighbourhoods. Modern work on witchcraft stresses not its irrationality, but the ways in which both beliefs and prosecutions could be a rational response to the challenges of early modern life.

Gender relations are integral to that picture, with women's domestic roles vulnerable to magical intervention, their reproductive expertise not dissimilar to magical powers, and ideas of female weakness correlated to susceptibility to the snares of the Devil. However, women played prominent roles not just as accused witches, but as accusers and witnesses. The English legal system, organized around grass-roots accusations rather than inquisitions, facilitated this kind of collaboration.

None of this means that witchcraft was not 'about' gender, but it makes for a more complex picture than a misogynistic attack on women by men, illuminating the significance of divisions and conflicts between women, and the ways that women were enlisted in a project of fear and confrontation which gave them some power over the intangible and unpredictable. Diane Purkiss urged historians to consider the psychic world of witches and their accusers. The dramas of witchcraft often took place in the world of women's work and care: around the house, over the cooking fire, in the rocking cradle, at the river where washing was done. They involved conflicts between women over the scarce resources of good housewifery. Much of the damage of witchcraft was an attack on the fragile process of producing edible food and drink, with particular attention to brewing, baking and cheese-making, all processes where corruption at a crucial point could make everything go wrong. Motherhood was also in question. The power of familiars recalls that of disruptive children and suggests the significance of maternity to witchcraft stories (Purkiss, 1995). In some narratives women turn the loss of children into stories of witchcraft; in many, witches threaten infants. Witchcraft confessions might even suggest the power that being suspected to be a witch might give women. At the same time, it is important to remember how many single women and widows, and how many old poor women, lived in English communities: single women were not automatically threatening, and witches were not necessarily isolated from communities, but integrated into them, often through networks of obligation and care that were easily upset. Cases of possession, by contrast, tended to involve more contained domestic dramas. These stories invoke a capacity to infringe both mental and physical boundaries, with a frightening significance for the children and young girls who were possessed, and the women who were thought to have possessed them.

Male witches seem to counter the trend. Some historians have characterized them as examples of failed masculinity; but they were described in terms of power and authority. While some were accused of the same kinds of maleficium as female witches, other men were prosecuted for sorcery, enchantment and charming, and they were not poor, but substantial men; some were working with book magic. Cases featuring professional identities, male expertise, and official power suggest that masculinity in its various presentations is critical to understanding male witchcraft (Kent, 2005).

## Popular Rituals

The communal nature of early modern life made popular judgement a key force in monitoring and shaping gender roles and relations. It was both a practical manifestation of the public nature of domestic life and an aspect of the way selfhood was experienced through relatedness and embeddedness. Moral offences brought shame, not just to an individual, but to a household, a street or a village. In response, communities mobilized rituals that exerted considerable force on gender relations. Supportive rituals endorsed transitional moments, such as those around childbirth: the gathering of women to help in labour and visit afterwards made 'gossips' figures of influence, and lying-in a time of gravity. Rituals of censure drew on powerful symbolic performances, illuminating a world where concrete objects and practices held deep meanings. The horns of cuckolds, supposedly derived from the fate visited in Greek mythology on Actaeon when he caught Artemis bathing, could be invoked in hand gestures like that indicated in the cover image, Jan Steen's painting *Celebrating the Birth*. Cuckoldry was the mark of men who had been unable to satisfy their wives or fooled by their deceit; other rituals targeted inversions of gender order.

In the skimmington ritual, best documented in the West Country, a man rode backwards on a horse being beaten by a 'wife', often a woman in men's clothes, sometimes using the skimming ladle women used for cheesemaking. Skimmington, or 'riding the stang' as it was also known in the north, provided an elaborate, well-established ritual for humiliating men who were allegedly subordinated to their wives, and wives who 'wore the breeches'. Rough music by a crowd beating pans and basins often accompanied it. Ballads and other narratives of gender disorder drew on these familiar images; a frieze of 'riding the stang' on the wall of the Great Hall at Montacute House, Somerset, commemorated it for visitors (Figure 3.1). In such rituals, gender regulation was materialized as well as symbolically invoked. Breeches, horns, skimming ladles, ducking stools and the often mentioned (but rarely seen) scold's bridle embodied well-known meanings and evoked the spectre of inversions of order, reinforcing the need for natural hierarchy.

Rituals like these were part of a Europe-wide festive tradition of **charivari**, overlapping with or standing in for formal justice. Magistrates, too, sentenced sexual offenders to ride in carts, or to be led about the town with basins being rung behind them. The ducking stools that parishes exerted themselves to buy at the turn of the sixteenth century were the folkloric punishment for scolds – women who disrupted the peace by aggressive speech. A classic article by David Underdown suggested a crisis of gender relations in the period 1560–1640, characterized by skimmingtons, the purchase of scolding stools, and witchcraft prosecutions. He also detected regional differences based on the established distinction between upland, woodland/pasturing regions (in the north and west) and downland, arable farming-based areas (in the south and east). Community rituals of punishment were more frequent in woodland/pasture uplands, where the economy depended on cheese-making and rural industry, and where settlements were dispersed, regulatory structures weak, and communities less cohesive. In the more traditional, nucleated settlements of the arable downlands, using open-field agriculture and where traditional structures of manor, squire and village government persisted, gender relations were more likely to feature pre-emptive social control and fewer punishments of women (Underdown, 1985). While the idea of a crisis in gender relations, suggesting earlier stability,

*Figure 3.1* Skimmington frieze in the Great Hall at Montacute House, Somerset, featuring a husband beaten by his wife made to ride on a broom. Plaster, *c.*1600.
© National Trust. Photographic Library/Nadia Mackenzie/Bridgeman Images.

has met with resistance, it does offer some useful opportunities for thinking about change, particularly in relation to patterns of women's work and poverty: the economic and social characteristics of upland parishes might have encouraged both women's agency, and popular concern about disorderly women (Weil, 2013). Other evidence suggests that prosecutions of scolds, which sometimes included men, varied in their nature and focus around the country. The role of economic development and regional differentiation in gender relations remains ripe for further examination.

While popular rituals of inversion are commonly read as conservative, the gender confrontations dramatized in popular culture had other meanings too. Ballads (and their woodcuts) rehearsed tales of comic female domination, self-respecting maids, murderous wives and warrior women using familiar tropes and a stock of recognizable tunes, some particularly identified with stories about women. But each performance would be shaped by the singer's voice and gestures, and many ballads invoked a female voice. Explicit confrontations about gender relations were one of the hallmarks of this period; they both reinforced order, and held the promise of change.

## Credit

The social bonds of early modern England were built on trust. In a culture still largely oral, the security of social relations depended on credit which was both moral and economic. Reputation was integral to community life, and it was fought out with words and blows [Doc. 38]. Women, especially vulnerable to sexual shaming, were often ready both to attack misconduct, and to defend themselves against discrediting words. Honesty for women was frequently interpreted as meaning sexual chastity; for men it encompassed financial and verbal honesty. These variable meanings gave the critical concept of credit a gendered edge.

The legal system gave ample support to the importance of reputation. Ordinary women and men pursued the defence of their good names in slander litigation, notably at the church courts, where common law constraints on women's legal status did not apply and large proportions of litigants were single and married women. The most conspicuously actionable words there were 'whore', 'bawd' and 'quean' for women, 'cuckold' and 'whoremaster' for men, suggesting a sharply divided culture of sexual blame in which men's sexual reputation depended on women's behaviour, and sexual unchastity was a symbol of corruption and poor character [Doc. 39].

The extent and rationale of the double sexual standard has been debated: men, it has been asserted, attracted blame too, though the ready language to condemn them for unchastity was never there. The biological reality of pregnancy, with paternity unprovable, facilitated a culture of anxiety about fatherhood; but the sexual blaming and shaming of women fulfilled a much bigger function of justifying the control of women and the fear of female deceit or betrayal.

Reputation applied not only to individuals, but to households and families. The economic significance of the household meant that the personal and domestic were entwined; husbands and wives, to a great extent, shared a joint credit. The logic of the double standard left men exposed to the impact of their wives' sexual conduct. The cultural response to this dilemma was the figure of the cuckold, resonant throughout Renaissance and Restoration culture as a target of ridicule and a focus of male anxiety. Like the language of whoredom, that of cuckoldry had a political import: civic rituals and protests used the images of cuckoldry to poke fun at certain trades, namely cobblers and tailors, and during times of unrest, against political victims.

Reputation was not just sexual, and gossip was not exclusively female. Men's defences of their reputation uncover another set of concerns which convey something of the culture of early modern masculinity. Accusations of lying, thieving, or abuse of office undermined male credit; financial honesty and artisanal skill gave men status and honour. In an expanding economy with increasingly fierce competition for resources, social credit was aligned with financial credit. London Puritan Nehemiah Wallington agonized over one exchange in his shop that might have shown him to be untrustworthy [**Doc. 40**]. Credit was a chain: trustworthiness depended not only on personal morality, but on the worth of those who were prepared to extend their trust. Young men's promotion in society and business required the goodwill of their peers, their seniors and their superiors. Credit was also established and undermined by words as well as transactions; gossip about bad business could undo a household.

The artisanal and financial aspects of credit engaged women as well as men, though there were significant obstacles, such as exclusion from guilds to women establishing occupational identity. Women ran households and businesses, took pride in their work, and described their capacity to make a living when questioned in court. Their credit was significant to local economies, and their names mattered to them. It seems likely, given the power of sexual insult for women, that sexual and economic credit combined for women in a way it did not for men.

## Friendship

The persistent elision of women's history, gender history and the history of the family performs a sleight of hand that erases a whole register of gender relations: that of friendship. In a fairly heterosocial world, relations between women and men were not bound to be sexual. And while it is critical to restore the sexual context of same-sex relations, early modern friendship had considerable capacity for physical intimacy that was not necessarily read as erotic.

Much work on friendship has focused on its instrumental aspects, particularly for men. Friendship between men was the root of patronage and clientage in political and spiritual matters as well as elite society. It encompassed a physical intimacy that made 'the gift of the body' part of social relationships: kisses, shared beds and tables, and loving letters embodied the social prestige of male homosociality (Bray and Rey, 1999: 68). At court and among gentry society, physical intimacy displayed personal and political connections. The largely unspoken opposite of those transactions was the crime of sodomy. For early modern men, the emotional and physical landscape of friendship contained an expansive terrain between homosociality and homoeroticism.

The political charge of female friendship between women was generally less visible, though the late seventeenth-century court featured some intense female networks, and the relationships between Queen Anne, **Sarah Churchill** and **Abigail Masham** erupted in scandalous conflict in the early eighteenth century. Epistolary friendships were celebrated among intellectual women, and in elite circles social relations between women could be an important conduit to patronage, or a source of bitter conflict.

With less money or power at stake, friendship must still have held both emotional and instrumental significance for the middling sort and the poor. The practice of chain migration that brought women and men to urban communities meant they often settled close to old connections from their birthplace, establishing new kinship networks. Looking for work, finding housing and making a marriage all depended on friends. Friend remained, though, a largely formal word, used in relation to family and kin, and often associated with the financial investments of business and marriage; the bonds of reciprocity that bound men and women together were often best described in the word 'neighbour'. A community of propinquity was also a network of moral obligations, in which gender relations were under constant scrutiny and in which women held a special stake. Women's invitations to gossipings after childbirth were a key element of the social currency of neighbourhood life, and featured in psychological anxieties expressed in dreams and astrological consultations; men's purchases of gloves for midwives and gossips brought them into the bonding ritual of reproduction too. Men's sociability sealed business deals and marriage contracts. Women's comradeship also had public contexts: marketplaces, church and weddings, and the feasting rituals at baptisms and churchings. Women, like men, built a neighbourhood of useful connections.

Among the young, sociability had its own gender dynamics. Legal records in courtship disputes suggest the importance of intimate confidences between women. Young men's comradeship was notorious for its excess: drinking, gaming and dancing were common complaints against apprentices (Figure 3.2). Male bonding rituals could also be disruptive to patriarchy. The drinking and fighting that bound men together and helped define male identity also posed a threat to civic and national order.

The post-Reformation impetus to spiritual self-examination encouraged friendships rooted in spiritual discussions, especially for literate women, increasingly identified as naturally inclined toward piety. Platonic friendship could be a way to explore deep intellectual and passionate connections with men as well as women. Margaret Blagge (later Godolphin), a maid of honour at the Restoration court, found in her six years' friendship and epistolary relationship with the diarist John Evelyn a haven in which to explore her religious commitment, and test her spiritual ideas (Harris, 2003) Such friendships made it possible for women to engage in intellectual adventure and to influence men without the constraints that physical presence might bring. Relationships between women and priests, often treated as

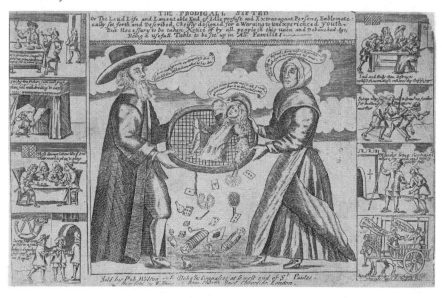

*Figure 3.2 The Prodigal Sifted.* A commonplace image of parents sieving their son of his vices, surrounded by images of gambling, duelling, drinking, smoking, a brothel, sickness and jail. Etching, 1677 (this impression 1740s), 19.7 cm × 30.6 cm.

suspicious, were crucial to maintaining Catholicism in post-Reformation England. Protestant women of elite status also developed bonds with ministers, of which letters and funeral sermons provide some memorials.

## Thinking Globally

Thinking globally about gender reveals the gendered dimensions of colonialism, imperialism and economic expansion. It also illuminates the engagement and roles of women as they moved across borders and, less directly, participated in trade, military and naval projects.

The colonial projects of early modern England and Britain ranged from Ireland to the Caribbean and the trading enterprises of the East India and Royal African Companies. In all these contexts, as in travel more generally, colonization created frontiers of gender, where different systems of knowledge and organization met (Brown, 1996: 33). Some English men in New England viewed matrilineal indigenous cultures as barbarous; some Native Americans saw English marital customs and gender roles as disorderly. Successful settlement, in Ireland and across the Atlantic, demanded respectable English women as transmitters of language and culture, as well as for marriage. To this end, single women were encouraged to emigrate to Virginia. Later, Quaker women found themselves seized by the reforming impulse to travel to spread their message in Manhattan, Barbados, or Malta, often recording their experiences in letters back home; for them, the will of God might provide a source of agency [**Doc. 33**]. Women also moved less voluntarily around the connected world of the British, captured and ransomed in pirate raids, forced into indentured servitude, and enslaved. A Black servant in Bristol escaped from her mistress's attempt to have her transported; a Portuguese woman, captured by north African pirates, ended up marrying the English merchant who had ransomed her and brought her back to London [**Doc. 6; Doc. 41**].

Women's active place in the transatlantic world challenges models of passivity and containment. Such roles were unrealistic for most women, and the colonial context demanded female agency. As well as travelling, women were economically engaged in the project of expansion and in the bureaucracy of empire. In trading companies like the East India Company, women were heavily involved in trading, lending, and accessing family credit: they petitioned, complained and confronted company authority. As wives and widows of sailors, women took charge of pay tickets, often accumulating dozens of them. When payments were obstructed, they combined to protest; as they engaged with naval bureaucracy, they became part of the enterprise of military expansionism (Hunt, 2004).

Research on the intersections between gender and the establishment of racialized slavery in the Caribbean and North America has laid particular stress on women's reproductive and labour roles, and the impact of the doctrine of *partus sequitur ventrem* (meaning that the condition of slavery follows the mother) laid down in Virginia in 1662 (Morgan, 2004). While the reach of those intersections in England is less clear, English men and women invested in slavery and brought enslaved women and men into their households. Concepts of law, race and gender travelled with planters, settlers and their families; for example, the expectation that white women did not labour in the fields may have fed into the eighteenth-century ideology of separate spheres (Amussen, 2007). English women travellers, notably Quakers, sometimes protested against slavery, but were as likely to accept it. Joan Vokins, travelling as a Quaker in Barbados and Antigua, spoke to separate congregations of white Quakers and Black slaves there, finding her soul 'melting' in both contexts but offering no contest to the segregation [**Doc. 33**]. Other archives can reveal important glimpses of Black men and women's resistance to slavery in England (Ewen, 2021).

# 4 Polity

The conventional political history of early modern England has had little to say about gender. Yet sexual politics were at the heart of political rhetoric and practice. The Tudor and Stuart commonwealth was frequently described as a mirror of a household, with the relationship between monarch and country reflected in that between the patriarch and his family – wife, children and servants. The political dramas of the Civil Wars, the Restoration, and the 1688 Revolution were accompanied by changing ideas that have been taken as key to political modernity: the development of social contract theory and ideas about the sovereignty of the people, and the distinction of private and public spheres. Gender and families were of continuing political significance, and political ideas drew on concepts of womanhood, manhood, family, marriage and legitimacy. Some of these were enduring and traditional; others were specific to the moment. Despite these changing ideas, it is hard to see permanent substantive change for women; the Whig 'liberal democracy' still rested on gender hierarchy.

Historians of gender and politics have made great progress in tracing the participation of women in spheres from which they were apparently excluded. From the earliest feminist historians of the nineteenth century, whose work enlisted a long history of women's political roles to support the contemporary cause of suffrage, through the Marxist and subsequent historians of protest, their interrogation of manuscript and print archives has illuminated women's participation in a variety of levels of political engagement. Framing politics around gender also illuminates the impact of changing political participation on masculinity, and the role of gender relations in political rhetoric. Debates invoking gender permeated every level of politics.

## Languages of Politics

The dominant political language of the seventeenth century was one of patriarchalism. In this theory, paternal political authority was part of the natural order. In the familiar Ten Commandments and elsewhere, the obligation for children to obey parents was directly linked to the subjects' duty to obey their monarch. The parallel comparison of conjugal authority to monarchs was more

DOI: 10.4324/9781003090786-6

problematic: wives were companions, not servants. Household advice and political theory presented domestic hierarchy as a microcosm of political order, and a training ground for it [**Doc. 27**]. During the political shifts of the seventeenth century these parallels were reconfigured to encompass patriarchal obligation and the potential of resistance, but remained a key resource for political thinking; Elizabeth Poole, a plebeian woman prophesying to the Army in 1649, drew on the language of patriarchalism to articulate her argument that the trial of the King should not lead to regicide [**Doc. 42**].

Reflecting the political meanings of gender, the rhetoric of sex permeated political discourse. Tyranny and Catholicism were typically cast as feminine; slurs of effeminacy and petticoat government were used to shame unpopular rulers. Insults like whore, cuckold and bawd permeated Reformation debates and Civil War banners and print. In debates on the conduct of the monarchy and the state, the role of women and the power of sex were constantly at issue. Popular demonstrations drew on gendered ideas of disorder. Always, the figure of *woman* stood alongside the acts of real women. Political historians have increasingly seen communication as central to understanding the conflicts of the seventeenth century; the gender of politics was the result of the public engagement of rhetoric with practical experience.

Seventeenth-century political thinkers and legislators were preoccupied with defining participation and rights. Often, this meant redefining concepts and groups to explicitly exclude women. As the concept of the individual became more defined, so did that of property. Holding land in freehold was becoming established as the measure of civic personhood, and the test for participation. The degree to which gender differentiated political participation is still under scrutiny. In part this is an issue of language: the false universal, where the term 'men' is used to mean people while excluding women, was an established feature of political discourse. Thomas Smith, describing the structure of government, explicitly excluded women, along with bondmen, from the office-holding that was accessible to most men [**Doc. 43**]. Citizenship was equated with manhood, maturity and capacity, all of which were identified as male. As the potential for imagining the greater participation of men in the polity appeared, the capacity to imagine female citizenship seemed to contract.

The narrative of a developing public sphere, defined as civic, male and rational, leaving women in a private, domestic world, is a central theme in women's history and gender history. In the late seventeenth century, spaces like coffee houses and media such as newspapers enabled people to commune politically as 'a public', distinct from the private, family world. Mapping gender roles onto those spheres, though, was an ongoing and contentious project. Women were figured as opponents to coffee houses, but they had a distinctive role in petitioning and pamphleteering, and a longstanding political voice, expressed in protest and sedition. The very exclusion of women from politics facilitated the voice of women's petitions, the narratives of wartime martyrdom, and the identification of women with mercy. At another level, the frequent invocation of 'ladies', 'virgins' and 'maids' in popular political literature made the female figure a key fantasy participant in political debate. Women's place in the polity was defined by conflicting and ambivalent cultural currents. Men's was less explicitly discussed in relation to gender, but political and religious changes also brought shifts in the relationship of masculinity to politics, making husbands and householders more clearly the embodiment of citizenship.

By the early seventeenth century, England had constituted itself rhetorically, culturally and politically as a nation. The national identity that developed in the sixteenth century and held sway through the seventeenth drew on deep-rooted ideas about gender. The Protestantism that provided a central bulwark of national identity was a domestic religion; but much of its ideological potency came from a political xenophobia. The anti-Catholicism that was an element of popular Protestantism had a powerful gender politics to it. Mary, Queen of Scots was one obvious target. In the early seventeenth century the Catholic threat was frequently linked to feminine government and tyranny; the Catholic queens of James I and Charles I provided lightning rods for popular anti-Catholicism, expressed for example by Lucy Hutchinson [Doc. 44]. The formation of national identity in relation to a foreign 'other' was also a project of gender.

## Monarchy

Monarchs were perceived as having two bodies, the mortal and the political; they also, Cynthia Herrup has argued, embodied two genders, the male and the female (Herrup, 2006). This was functional for both male and female monarchs. Elizabeth I referred to herself as a prince, while Mary I's funeral displayed the gauntlet and spurs of a military leader. The duality of kingship also had a gendered aspect: kings had to balance martial rigidity with tender mercy, while avoiding the perception of 'feminine' tyranny or inconstancy.

The issue of queens regnant was a recurrent feature of Tudor and Stuart politics. Much historiography has focused on the gender politics of Elizabeth I's position. She developed a style of self-presentation, from speeches to portraits, that drew on such diverse elements as virginity, princehood and maternity; meanwhile some of her plebeian subjects used sexual insult to slander her. Mary I had previously negotiated some of the same dilemmas, but also the issue of her duty to conjugal obedience to her husband, a foreign prince, who was granted the title of King for his lifetime only.

For all the female monarchs of this period, the ability of a woman to rule a country was less in question than the negotiation of her marital status and the religion of her potential or actual husband. If a queen, once married, became a feme covert like any other woman, many of her rights in her own name vanished; lawyers of Mary I's reign suggested that marriage would imperil her capacity to hold the crown and bequeath it to her heir. The strategies of queens negotiating the place of power derived both from having a female body on a throne, and from broader dynastic and political strategies. The domestic nature of monarchical government was also an issue. A queen regnant brought with her a household of women, who could not be given the political posts that a king's male household would have; nevertheless, the women of the household and the bedchamber had significant political roles.

Reproductive politics were persistently an issue for Tudor and Stuart monarchs. The desperation with which Henry VIII attempted to consolidate his inheritance was followed by a series of dynastic crises in which the monarchy was faced with queens regnant, queens marrying foreigners, and queens with no heirs. Inheritance became still more complex in the later seventeenth century, with the fears of Catholic heirs, such as the son of James II, to the Protestant throne. When James II fled the throne in 1689 and William of Orange invaded, ostensibly to support his wife Mary's hereditary right to the crown, their lack of children was a positive advantage in avoiding the issue of subsequent succession. In the negotiations over the throne's settlement, the unfitness of a woman to rule was raised again. William expressed himself reluctant to be subordinate to his wife, and Mary appeared to readily accept the need for what one pamphlet called a 'vigorous and masculine administration' (Weil, 1999: 106). Following this principle, crowning the couple jointly, with the administration of the kingdom bestowed on William alone, resolved some of the difficulty of Mary's hereditary claim. The actual balance of their powers remained confusing.

On the throne, queens have always had a gender; that of kings has rarely been noticed. The dynastic struggles of Henry VIII, the passionate favouritism of James I and the alleged subordination of Charles II to the sexual power of women are all worth examining through the lens of masculinity. The divisions of the civil war also reflected ideas of manhood and power: the very different expressions of masculinity by Charles I, Cromwell and Charles II suggest some deep fissures in the notion of manhood.

## Participation

The formal mechanisms of government included little popular participation, and so the question of the qualification of women to participate in government was rarely discussed. The radicals of the English Revolution brought participation into question. However, when the Levellers and the New Model Army discussed the participation of commoners in the commonwealth at the Putney Debates of 1647, the commoners in question were universally taken to be male. Very few men and women in early modern England expected to participate actively in the polity in terms that are consonant with modern political identity: a minority participated in elections and members of Parliament came generally from an established elite. English women and men did, however, understand themselves to be political subjects of the monarch, of the government, and members of the church. The obligations of those roles were sometimes in dispute. The political dramas of the sixteenth and seventeenth centuries put the role of subject under sharp scrutiny. Women were unlikely to see themselves as political actors, but so were most men. Moreover, by the late seventeenth century the impact of the penal laws was to make Catholic men almost as legally disempowered as married women.

Historians and political theorists have seen in the late seventeenth century a process of excluding women formally from political participation, closing the loopholes that previously existed in customary practice. From the mechanisms of parliamentary selection to political theory, politics was being decisively identified as masculine. That formalization of exclusion meant not that women were depoliticized, but that their relationship to politics was likely to be expressed in complex ways: this might be demonstrated both through writing, and in words and actions.

Voting illuminates the difference between modern and early modern politics, and the complexity of tracing early modern women's participation. The capacity to vote for parliamentary representation is a touchstone of modern political engagement, and the first historians of early modern women's political roles, writing in the early twentieth century, were also interested in female suffrage. They searched out piecemeal evidence of the long history of women voting and participating in local governance. In this narrative, the seventeenth century represented the moment when women's historic freedoms were constricted, alongside economic marginalization.

The medieval statutes that defined the workings of parliamentary selection did not exclude women from participating in elections to parliament on the same basis as men, as freeholders holding land worth forty shillings or more. At least three legal cases in the reign of James I upheld the right of single women to vote for parliamentary representatives; if married, their husbands were to have their votes. Not all contemporaries recognized this. There is, however, evidence that participation in the process of election was not defined as exclusively male until the late seventeenth century.

Early modern elections were nothing like modern voting. Members of Parliament were chosen by a process more akin to selection than election, in which, for most of this period, consensus was a mark of a successful political process. Consequently, the voices of electors and selectors are particularly hard to trace. Typically, elections proceeded without an outright contest; the influence of propertied women might be both uncontroversial and invisible. In the 1640s, when contests became more likely, the right of women to cast a vote became controversial. Sir Edward Coke's treatise on the common law mentions, in passing, women's incapacity to vote for members of Parliament; at an election in Ipswich in 1640, votes from single women freeholders were first taken, then rejected on the basis that they were legal, but dishonourable to use. More significant than the numbers of women who 'voted' before 1660 was the lack of any structures forbidding them to do so.

After 1660, those structures began to be put into place through the redrawing of charters and the establishment of more predictable voting practices. There is no evidence of women voting in the elections of the late seventeenth century, and in 1690 Coke's exclusion of women was quoted, seemingly uncontroversially, in George Petyt's *Lex parliamentaria*. Voting had become, apparently without question, a male prerogative. But the significance of that prerogative was confined to the limited numbers of men who held sufficient property to vote. Arguably, property remained more significant than gender in enfranchisement.

Other political activities provide a better measure of gendered participation. The divided loyalties of the mid-seventeenth century brought a series of public tests for householders, such as the **Protestation Oath** in 1641–2 and the **Solemn League and Covenant** in 1643. Women are recorded as subscribing to these, in numbers that vary greatly by parish and oath. In some places all adult householders seem to have taken an oath; in one London parish up to half of the subscribers to the Solemn League and Covenant were female; in others the only women who subscribed were widows. Scottish women had played a prominent role in opposition to Charles I's prayer book, and many swore and some signed the **National Covenant** in 1638. While female influence was often characterized as a dangerous aspect of royalism, female protest and loyalty had a place in the national Parliamentarian cause.

## Resistance

The political consensus of early modern England involved a degree of acceptable protest, along with intermittently and unpredictably severe responses to demonstrations perceived as riots. Petitions and protests were one element of the relationship between subject and state, reflecting consensus, negotiation, and subordination. An established set of understandings about gendered responsibilities and roles determined women's and men's behaviour in crowds and protests. Habitually described, in court, as 'riot' or 'riotous', much of that behaviour was conventional and its ritual confrontations were part of the consensus that maintained authority. The local complaints that led to protest were also a conduit for national political issues.

As in other political arenas, the participation of women was both an accepted aspect of the politics of protest and a marker of disorder. The conventions of protest prescribed certain roles and powers for men and women. The language of patriarchalism at the heart of so much political discourse was also used in protest, enabling both women and men to engage with national politics: as the subjects of a patriarchal monarch, they were owed protection, as well as being obligated to obedience. Religion and conscience were the basis for protests about legitimate authority: the Henrician regime executed a number of women whose verbal resistance to religious reform was interpreted as treason. Women's role in provisioning the household and as mothers provided a rationale for participation in food riots and peace petitions. All these traditions made gender relations matter to protest.

The staging and prosecution of protest brought the issue of women's legal liability to the fore. Custom had long held that women were not legally responsible for damage in such cases, a principle that was reiterated in legal texts and in popular discourse. Sometimes men dressed as women to protest; sometimes women led riots and assumed the title 'Captain'. Events such as the hanging of 'Captain' Ann Carter after her leadership of the second Maldon riots in 1629 proved this belief in unaccountability to be utterly misconceived. In the Henrician period in particular, the degree of licence allowed to women's sedition and protest was dramatically uncertain. But the idea that women were somehow protected remained a feature of popular political culture through the first half of the seventeenth century, adding another dimension to the figure of the disorderly woman.

Food was a familiar ground of protest for women: in sixteenth- and seventeenth-century England they protested over scarcity, high prices or the quality of grain, and their collective and individual voices readily represented the claims of providers for hungry families. Recent interpretations describe food protests as a form of negotiation, rather than desperation, and female involvement should be seen in that light. Women participated not just because it was an emergency of subsistence; they expected to bargain through demonstration. Enclosure protests were more conspicuously male, but still featured women pulling down fences, destroying ditches and throwing stones. The protests on Grewelthorpe Moor, near Ripon in Yorkshire, in 1612 involved a number of middle-aged women, led by 'Captain Dorothy' Dawson, who broke down the new ditches erected to enclose the common land. Their responses clarify the defence offered by women accused of protest. They insisted they went 'two by two' – not, in other words, riotously; that no one person had led them; and that their husbands had not known what they were doing. Dawson's deposition, by far the longest, describes at length her defence of a poor woman who needed the grazing on the land to live [**Doc. 45**].

The precise balance of gender roles in protests is complicated by the politics of court reportage. Given the issue of female culpability, legal questions were often asked about whether women took part alone or with their husbands. Historians' interpretations have sometimes underplayed the leadership of women, and read their participation as figureheads for the grievances of men. The leadership of protests was far more likely to be by men than women, but partly because of the role that cross-dressing and gender politics played in such demonstrations, it was one of the places where men and women seemed to claim equivalent or parallel voices. When they were questioned, women protesters articulated a claim to protest for themselves, their families and the community. The more subtle analyses of early modern politics, and the rethinking of the state, that have emerged with recent historiography make it hard to dismiss any crowd action, however local in focus, as lacking in ideological depth or political nous. The right of women to protest over economic want, and to defend their families, gave them a lasting political voice, whose echoes continued to be felt first in the activism of the Civil War years, and later in the female-dominated food riots of the eighteenth and nineteenth centuries.

Muttering beneath the explicit petitions and protests were the exchanges of political conversation. In a highly oral culture, seditious words were a serious matter and, particularly before 1640, they were severely punished. But no government could control the constant flow of political debate. That monarchs and magistrates even attempted to do so testifies to the significance of speech in popular politics. Seditious words provide extensive evidence of the political voices of women, spreading scandalous claims about heresy, sexual misconduct, and corruption in government; they suggest a sphere of political discussion in which a wide range of people participated.

On the evidence of prosecutions, seditious words often highlighted sexual misconduct, with ordinary people spreading malicious rumours about their rulers. Elizabeth I was sometimes alleged to have had children by Leicester, which in some versions she had ordered to be killed and hidden in a chimney. While gossip was habitually characterized as female, sedition was a crime of both sexes, and inattention to women's speech may have meant that seditious words from women were actually less likely to be prosecuted. Much of what appears in the archival record concerns brief words, presented as single utterances. In reality, the danger of sedition was that, in a largely oral culture, it was also news. It spread fast, and it was remembered.

Clearly, women and men talked politics together, and political sedition was a sphere of discourse in which both sexes participated. They may have stressed different aspects; women seem to have been notably, though by no means exclusively, active in sexual rumours and stories about secret births or infertility. That, after all, was understood to be their special sphere of expertise. But women also voiced complaints about tax and war. Oral culture gave ordinary women and men a kind of political voice.

**Recusancy** had its own sexual politics. Contemporaries often suggested, and historians have agreed, that English Catholicism survived through the work of women. In the domestic realm Catholic women sheltered priests and preserved the material objects of the mass; in the outer world, it was often postulated, they attended church for conformity to shelter the recusancy of their husbands. Married women's recusancy fundamentally challenged the household-state analogy. Successive penal laws grappled with the difficulty of punishing wives who could not legally hold property, establishing ways to fine them and attempting to hold husbands responsible. Anti-Catholic rhetoric drew on the conventional image of the disorderly wife, compelling the henpecked husband to shelter her dissent.

## Civil War and Revolution

The exceptional activities of women in the 1640s and 1650s have long provided a high point of female activism for historical memory; more recent histories have expanded the political sphere to include the worlds of news, local politics and popular opinion, making room for a deeper politics of gender.

Attacks on Charles I's poor governance drew on gendered anxieties. His failure to govern the country was matched by his failings as a familial patriarch, and his submission to his over-dominant French and Catholic wife. More broadly, concerns about unruly women, gender inversion, and moral collapse were repeated features of the cultural landscape of the decades before the Civil War, as were the distinctions drawn between two types of men – honest countrymen and corrupt, foppish courtiers (Amussen, 2021). Gender debates were political debates.

During wartime, necessity and innovation shifted gender roles in practice. With 25–33 per cent of the adult male population mobilized, the relationship of masculinity to war was dramatically recast. The armies that fought the civil wars represented a new kind of organization; it was the first time for generations that Englishmen had armed themselves and fought on their home soil. The parliamentary armies constituted a departure from all previous military structures. Men were supposed to be advanced on merit; they prayed and fasted together; their victories came from God. Together they worked out a new kind of militaristic and egalitarian masculinity, in aspiration at least.

Women's engagement in the civil wars also expanded their familiar realm of action. Soldiers billeted on households throughout the country meant a wide range of families dealt with military men and their weapons, including guns, in their houses. Women were embedded in military life, working for example as provisioners and medical practitioners. In cities and towns, women defended fortifications, and in Norwich women sold their jewellery to fund a 'Maiden Troop'. Elite women found themselves defending houses and castles against besieging forces. When, in 1643, Brilliana Harley was facing the siege of her house at Brampton Bryan, her letters show her bringing the role of obedient wife into unison with the defence of Parliament and what she understood to be the true religion [**Doc. 46**]. The story of women's radicalism became part of revolutionary legend.

Like the Reformation, the civil wars were a battle of conscience that could divide husband and wife. For the majority, loyalty was regional: royalism was strongest in the north and west, parliamentarianism in the south and east. But as the possibility of consensus receded, opinions and convictions proliferated. The political storms of the early seventeenth century were accompanied by an outbreak of news. Through the 1640s, newsbooks were published regularly and circulated nationally; there was plenty of room for sectarian debate, and a growing audience for it. While the loyal support of wives leant ammunition to the weapons of both sides, husbands and wives did not always speak with one voice, and religious radicals both male and female had a spiritual justification for leaving the ties of family to follow the Lord. Revolution, like reformation, could provoke divisive dilemmas for married life.

The radical religious sects of the 1640s were renowned for their high levels of female participation. At least 300 women prophets can be identified through their printed works, two-thirds of them Quakers. Women prophets both defied and reinforced the conventions of gender. Identifying themselves as prophets like the men of the Old Testament, they spoke in a trance, sometimes using male voices, and claiming to articulate the voice of God. In that sense, they spoke out more audibly and with fewer constraints than most seventeenth century women were able to. Elizabeth Poole was received with acclaim by Cromwell and his Army Council, and reminded them of the importance of listening to her logically argued, biblically informed words. At the same time, the governing principle of female prophecy was that it emerged from, and was justified by, the idea of the 'weaker vessel': 'God hath chosen the foolish things of the world to confound the wise' (1 Corinthians 1:27). Prophecy was described as a forcible overwhelming by God's word; to attribute self-conscious self-assertion to women of the sects can miss the essential nature of seventeenth-century spirituality. Nevertheless, the result was a public space in which women's voices were heard, considered and discussed.

Male prophets were sometimes more radical in crossing gender roles, speaking of themselves as nursing mothers, as warriors and as babies, using metaphors of sex and the body that most women shrank from. Masculinity might give them a freedom that allowed them to challenge social order more deeply than their female counterparts. An exchange of letters between the **Ranter** leader, Abiezer Coppe and one of his female followers is revealing: while she dreams of growing strong like an eagle, it is he who insists there is no difference between male and female in Christ [**Doc. 47**]. The voice of male prophets often drew on authority, while that of women tended to be characterized by a tone of alienation.

Prophesying was never mainstream; it remained, for many, upsetting, offensive or plain wrong. But it should be seen in the light of two important strands of the early modern polity. One was the historic spiritual role of women, which endowed them with a special intuition to the divine. The prophets of the 1640s and 1650s were the heirs of Elizabeth Barton, the poor woman who prophesied to Henry VIII and his ministers in the 1530s, and they reaped both positive and ill effects from the long history of female visionaries. The other was the enlarged political sphere of the mid-seventeenth century. The new public of the 1640s was built on the growing circulation of and interest in national and international news. Women's literacy was quite sufficient to enable them to consume newsbooks; the increased flow of print and news and the lack of censorship that characterized the 1640s must have enlarged reading habits, particularly in urban communities. In the new print marketplace, large numbers of women's prophetic writings were published; it was the moment when women authors became mainstream. The voice of women in the politics of the 1640s left its fullest record in the petitions to parliament, presented by groups describing themselves as wives, maids or honest gentlewomen. They often advocated for peace, and for an end to wartime disruptions of trade, communities and families, but they also put their voices behind specific political and religious agendas. Such petitions drew on the long history of women protestors, who had traditionally assumed responsibility for the supply of food: subsistence was the common preoccupation of most of the petitions. Women petitioners also deployed the rhetoric of anti-Catholicism, hostility towards the episcopacy, and the investment of mothers in peace and national security.

Petitioning gave women a physical presence in the political world of Westminster: petitioners habitually gathered in a large crowd on the steps of parliament, outside the doors and in Westminster House. Some demonstrations became violent, such as that in 1643, and some resulted in arrests. Members of Parliament rarely responded positively to women's demonstrations; **Pym** notoriously told one group to go back to their houses [**Doc. 48**]. Critical newsbook accounts described the female crowds, in one instance reported to number five thousand, as composed of whores, bawds, oysterwomen and beggars. By 1646, demonstrations of women were most often associated with the Leveller cause, often on behalf of imprisoned men and women. Leveller women complained their domestic sphere had been violated by forceful arrest, echoing the politicization of women's roles that appeared in earlier petitions.

The idea of a political collective of women, hanging about on the stairs of parliament, is so pervasive in revolutionary rhetoric that it is hard to pin down how many and how often women were involved, and how significant their sex was in practice. Mixed and male public gatherings were seemingly less worthy of comment. But the female crowd was also significant because, however familiar the political voice of women, it signified disorder and spatial promiscuity.

The actual participation of women in public politics in the 1640s was paralleled by a parody of gender relations which drew on and revivified the old stereotypes of disorderly women, concerned only with sex. A series of 'Parliaments of Women' pamphlets took the petitioning activities of London women and turned them into an extended jest about women using parliament to legislate for cuckoldry. The habitual representation of the people as a subordinate wife, and the monarch as a masterful husband, made domestic relations an excellent register for political comment. The Puritan concern with sexual morality provided as much fodder for satire as the actual misdeeds alleged of sectarian groups. Newsbooks reported on the supposed sexual misconduct of prominent men on both sides, or claimed that London women were running wild out of men's control. In popular print, pornographic fantasy was blurred with gossip to libel public figures; news was both sexual and political. Virtuous virgins had political currency too. A petition of 1660, 'The Royall Virgine. Or the Declaration of Several Maydens', claimed to be printed for Virgin Hope-well, and sold at the Maiden-Starre, deploying the idea of maidenly virtue to disclaim the dishonourable behaviour of the **Rump Parliament.**

Within a few years, the public role of women in the Commonwealth had become more parody than real. The influence of women on royal government was identified as dangerous, provoking intrigue and mistrust. The long-running discourse of anti-Catholicism shaded femininity with misgovernment, tyranny and popery. In contrast, Parliamentarian politics drew on fraternal and civic connections, and on the shared world of men who had been in parliament and in the army together (Hughes, 2011). The new style of government meant men working together in a meritocracy; it did not mean men working with women. The most radical female voices had been in the sects but over time, those voices were marginalized and characterized as eccentric and unreliable precisely because of their articulation of a conscience that was once authentic, and swiftly became dangerous. The Restoration in 1660 has been seen as a reinstatement of male political authority, with greater constraints on women's political voice. As a basis for equality, spiritual claims proved unreliable.

The English Revolution, then, saw radical challenges to gender order, and new roles for both women and men. But it did not permanently transform gender relations. Even in the radical sects, the interactions of men and women often fell back into familiar patterns: women acting as 'mothers in Israel', organizing and facilitating, while men made the boldest ventures. In some marriages, the wars brought new divisions of labour; women like Brilliana Harley and Lucy Hutchinson give an insight into conjugal political thinking that must have played out in other contexts too. For the Harleys, as for other couples, another pattern also emerged: husbands' absence and wives' responsibility. More than relations between the sexes, relations within them were changed. The actions of women in the 1640s and 1650s drew on a new political collectivity of women; men's political roles drew on civic brotherhood. The old ceremonies of marriage and baptism were missed, and even when new forms were developed, the essence of marriage was unchanged. The fantasies of sexual disorder and gender overturned were more powerful than the reality.

## Social Contract and Sexual Contract

The political theories of seventeenth-century England often put the family at the centre of politics. The questions of authority and subordination, loyalty and resistance which loomed so large in the early modern state resonated with strains in familial relations. Marriage contracts, parental responsibilities, inheritance and adultery all had political meanings, and made for stirring connections between household and polity; when women wrote publicly about families, households, and gender politics, they might also be writing about the state and the national church. The Puritan gentlewoman Dorothy Leigh's popular work of maternal advice, *The Mother's Blessing*, was bound by one book buyer with a parallel but very different *Father's Blessing*, a popularized version of James I's *Basilikon Doron*; Leigh's text promoted the mother as spiritual adviser to the nation (Gray, 2001) [**Doc. 29**].

In the mid and late seventeenth century, the questions of legitimacy and resistance that were pivotal in national politics continued to have ties to the politics of the family. Whether, and how, a woman was subject to a man; how her subjection could, or should, be compelled; and whether their contractual relationship could ever be dissolved remained matters of great political import. The family/state parallel added an edge to the events of the 1640s and especially the regicide of 1649. The English Revolution brought an obvious parallel that worked both ways: while political rebellion against an alleged tyrant could be compared to the right of an abused wife to resist or divorce her husband, the act of regicide was treason comparable to the petty treason of husband-murder, or even, in Elizabeth Poole's formulation, the severance of the head from the body [**Doc. 42**]. The late seventeenth century saw further contests to the parallel between household and state, but the connections between family and politics still mattered. Political parties in parliament emerged in part in response to a crisis of family inheritance: the emerging Whig party's attempts, in 1685, to exclude Charles II's brother James, a convert to Catholicism, from the throne challenged the meaning of inheritance and legitimacy. The 'warming pan scandal' of 1688 involved a print furore and a public fantasy about the illegitimacy of the Catholic heir to the throne. Rumours circulated that Mary of Modena had never been pregnant at all, and that the child had been smuggled into her bed in a warming pan; the equivocation of the best witnesses, midwives and women at court helped the story stick. The unrelated crime of Mary Hobry, a French midwife who was burnt for the murder of her husband in the same year, was drawn into the rhetoric of women's dangerous part in Catholic conspiracy; the alleged role of Elizabeth Cellier, 'the popish midwife', in the popish plots of 1679 had a similar effect. The public authority of women in the drama of reproduction was at the heart of the political crisis of the 1680s.

The political developments of the later seventeenth century undercut the long-cherished political theory of patriarchalism. At the beginning of our period, the political order was commonly explained by analogy: the authority of the king was comparable to that of a father in a household. From this root came much of the domestic advice of the Puritan reformers, as well as the understanding of the household as a public concept. By the end of the seventeenth century, the patriarchalist vision was eclipsed by those of Hobbes, Locke and others, in which political authority was dependent on the consent of the governed in a social contract. The rise of social contract theory was associated, in varying degrees depending on historians' views, with the Revolution of 1688, when James II was deemed to have abdicated to be replaced by William of Orange and his wife, James's daughter Mary.

The political meaning of the 1688 revolution and its relationship to a modern polity remains in contest. Feminist historians have interrogated its implications for gender in relation to the impact of social contract on theories of the family, and to the various configurations of the politics of family life in the late seventeenth century. Carole Pateman argued that the social contract of Locke continued dependent on an implicit 'sexual contract', in which women were subjected to men (Pateman, 1988). The civil freedom that contract establishes is, in this formulation, a masculine freedom, and it brings with it a continuation of the same order that underlay patriarchalism. The absence of any discussion of that sexual contract in contract theory means it can be presumed to be natural – more so than it was in patriarchalism. The putative liberalism of the Whigs thus emerges as at least as socially conservative as patriarchalism, with the further consequence of privatizing family life. At the same time, Whigs and Tories, contractarians and patriarchalists held a diversity of views about female roles and marriage. The high-profile dramas of succession put marriage and inheritance at the centre of public debate: no clear line could be drawn around the privacy of the family, nor could gender be fenced off from public discussion.

# 5 Conclusion

## Assessment

In early modern England as in other times and places, powerful forces maintained an equilibrium of inequality. Gender historians, of necessity, track the obstacles to change as well as the potentials for movement. There were a surprising number of voices for change in early modern England, as well as significant structural shifts, some temporary, some more permanent. One key shift was in the economic and social context of marriage, a key determinant of women's experiences. The world in which households were the key unit of work, society and religion, as well as sex and reproduction, was changing, particularly in urban communities; both women and men had more options of separate work lives and social identities, while religious identities were fractured. Single life was more common and more economically feasible. At the same time, the decreased capacity for intensive moral scrutiny and the growing idea of domestic privacy for the middling sort separated marriage and family from the public sphere. In some ways, this limited women's lives; it may also have posed risks, as marital violence became a private issue.

Religious change intersected importantly with gender. The introduction of Protestantism, the growth of Puritanism, the persecution of Catholics and the fracturing of religious identities in the seventeenth century all impacted on gendered roles and gender relations. While the fundamental message of womanly duties, chastity and virtue remained consistent, the roles women played in spiritual practice altered; the religious rituals around childbirth were challenged, and reproduction was imbued with political and religious significance; and a gendered language provided the means of articulating religious conflict, crisis and nurture. In times of religious conflict, women's voices were often more clearly heard. The stories of argumentative Protestant female martyrs came to be a resource for the debating radical women of a hundred years later, in a moment at which female conscience was understood to represent the voice of God and the concerned nation.

Politically, the evidence suggests women's roles were more, not less, constrained by 1700; monarchical government had room for a few powerful women in a way that parliamentary representation could not yet allow. But in intellectual networks, in feminist thought, in petitions and in political discussion, the range of women's ideas, supported by a new wave of education for girls of the

DOI: 10.4324/9781003090786-7

middling sort and gentry, was expansive, and the capacity to express them in print and in writing was much enlarged.

What of the foundations of sexual and gender difference? The elements of biblical teaching, tradition, family life, and community pressure that shaped gender roles shifted in emphasis and to a degree in their nature. Historians place much less stress on community rituals after 1640: the figures of witches, scolds and cuckolds and rituals like skimmingtons or rough music are much less in evidence, and in urban areas a different kind of community life had developed. By 1700, hierarchy and tradition did not prevent Judith Drake from asserting that women and men could be equal [**Doc. 24**].

The regularization of legal and political structures tended to also regularize women's exclusion or subordination. The complex legal system of overlapping jurisdictions included considerable room for female manoeuvre, through customary law, ecclesiastical law, manorial courts, and equity jurisdictions like the relatively accessible Court of Common Pleas. All, by 1700, were losing place to the common law, where coverture was rigidly enforced. A relatively flexible legal system was giving way to a more systematic one, and the constraints on married women were beginning to rouse feminist complaint.

Across these contexts of body, mind, family, community and polity, there was an equilibrium of inequality. Changing ideologies of masculinity and femininity and new possibilities for community and work did not alter the underlying conviction of male superiority and female subordination, with all its economic, social, political and personal ramifications. But there were also challenges, transformations, and shifts of power in which women, individually and collectively, made change happen.

# Part II

# Documents

# Document 1

## *Jane Anger*

*Jane Anger's pamphlet in defence of women was one of the earliest contributions to the English 'querelle des femmes'. Addressed 'to the gentlewomen of England', it countered a previous pamphlet's insults of women and set forth some familiar, and some novel, defences of the virtues of women. There is no evidence that Anger was her real name, or even that she was a woman.*

The creation of man and woman at the first, he being formed in principio of dross and filthy clay, did so remain until God saw that in him his workmanship was good, and therefore by the transformation of the dust which was loathsome unto flesh, it became purified. Then lacking a help for him, God making woman of men's flesh, that she might be purer than he, does evidently show, how far we women are more excellent than men. Our bodies are fruitful, whereby the world increases, and our care wonderful, by which man is preserved. From woman sprang man's salvation. A woman was the first that believed, and a woman likewise the first that repented sin. In women is only true fidelity: (except in her) there is constancy, and without her no huswifery. In the time of their sickness we cannot be wanted, and when they are in health we for them are most necessary. They are comforted by our means: they nourished by the meats we dress: their bodies freed from diseases by our cleanliness, which otherwise would surfeit unreasonably through their own noisomeness. Without our care they lie in their beds as dogs in litter, and go like lousy mackerel swimming in the heat of summer. They love to go handsomely in their apparel, and rejoice in the pride thereof, yet who is the cause of it, but our carefulness, to see that every thing about them be curious. Our virginity makes us virtuous, our conditions courteous, and our chastity maketh our trueness of love manifest.

Source: *Jane Anger Her Protection for Women* (1589), sig. C1–C1v.

# Document 2

## *Levinus Lemnius*

*Dutch physician Levinus Lemnius's 400-page* The Secret Miracles of Nature *was first published in Antwerp in 1559, and translated into English a hundred years later. Offering both a philosophical and an anatomical discussion of the body and nature, it was quite influential and a source for subsequent works, notably the sex guide/midwives' book known as* Aristotle's Masterpiece. *This extract is from a chapter in Book IV entitled 'Of the Nature of Women'.*

For a woman's mind is not so strong as a man's, nor is she so full of understanding and reason and judgement, and upon every small occasion she casts off the bridle of reason, and like a mad dog, forgetting all decency, and her self, without choice, she sets upon all, be they known or unknown. If any man desires a natural reason for it, I answer him thus, that a woman's flesh is loose, soft and tender, so that the choler being kindled, presently spreads all the body over, and causeth a sudden boiling of the blood about the heart. For as fire soonest take hold of light straw, and makes a great flame, but it is soon at an end, and quieter; so a woman is quickly angry and flaming hot, and rageth strangely; but this rage and crying out, is soon abated, and grows calm in a body that is not so strong and valiant, and that is more moist; and all her heat and fury is quenched by her shedding of tears, as if you should throw water upon fire to put it out. Which we see also in some effeminate men, whose magnanimity and fierceness ends almost as children's do in weeping, when the adversary doth strongly oppose himself against them. If any man would more nearly have the cause of this thing explained, and desires a more exact reason; I can find no nearer cause that can be imagined, than the venom and collection of humours, that she every month heaps together, and purgeth forth by the course of the moon; For when she chanceth to be angry, as she will presently be, all that sink of humours being stirred fumeth, and runs through the body, so that the heart and brain are affected with the smoky vapours of it, and the spirits both vital and animal, that serve those parts are inflamed, and thence it is that women stirred up, especially the younger women (for the elder that are past childing, are more quiet and calm, because their **terms** are ended) will bark, and brawl like mad dogs, and clap their hands and behave themselves very unseemly in their actions and speeches, and reason being but weak in them, and their judgement feeble, and their mind not well ordered, they are sharply enraged, and cannot rule their passions. And the baser any woman is in that sex, the more she scolds and rails, and is unplacable in her anger, hence the vulgar women and whores (for noble women and gentlewomen will usually observe a decorum, though oft times they will be silent, and bend their brows, and scarce vouchsafe to give their husbands an answer, the Dutch call it *Proncken*) because their bodies are commonly polluted with faulty humours, are full of impudence, joined with equal malice, as if the Devil drove them, and they cannot be persuaded by counsel, reason, shame, flattery, admonition (that will ordinarily make wild beasts quiet) and you cannot hold them from their cruelty, or make them forbear their mad and loud exclamations.

Source: Levinus Lemnius, *The Secret Miracles of Nature: in Four Books* (1658), pp. 274–5.

## Document 3

### Jane Sharp

*Jane Sharp's guide to childbirth, published in 1671 and dedicated 'To the Mid-wives of England', was the first such book in English by a woman. Its view of the female body drew on classical and sixteenth century sources, with some original interjections. Matrix: womb; Cod: scrotum; Yard, penis; Stones, testicles.*

## Book I, Chap. XII 'Of the Likeness of the Privities of Both Sexes'

But to handle these things more particularly, *Galen* saith that women have all the parts of Generation that Men have, but Men's are outwardly, women's inwardly.

The womb is like to a man's Cod, turned the inside outward, and thrust inward between the bladder and the right Gut, for then the stones which were in the Cod, will stick on the outsides of it, so that what was a Cod before will be a Matrix, so the neck of the womb which is the passage for the Yard to enter, resembleth a Yard turned inwards, for they are both one length, only they differ like a pipe, and the case for it; so then it is plain, that when the woman conceives, the same members are made in both sexes, but the Child proves to be a Boy or a Girl as the seed is in temper; and the parts are either thrust forth by heat, or kept in for want of heat; so a woman is not so perfect as a Man, because her heat is weaker, but the Man can do nothing without the woman to beget Children, though some idle Coxcombs will needs undertake to shew how Children may be had without use of the woman.

## Book II, Chap. 1 'What Things Are Required for the Procreation of Children'

The two principles then that are necessary in this case are the seed of both sexes, and the mother's blood; the seed of the Male is more active than that of the Female in forming the creature, though both be fruitful, but the female adds blood as well as seed out of which the fleshy parts are made, and both the fleshy and spermatick parts are maintain'd and preserv'd. What *Hippocrates* speaks of two sorts of Seed in both kinds, strong and weak seed, hot and cold, is to be understood only of strong and weak people, and as the seed is mingled, so are boys and girls begotten.

The Mother's blood is another principle of children to be made; but the blood hath no active quality in this great work, but the seed works upon it, and of this blood are the chief parts of the bowels and the flesh of the muscles formed, and with this both the spermatical and fleshy parts are fed; this blood and the menstrual blood, or monthly Terms are the same, which is a blood ordained by Nature for the procreation and feeding of the Infant in the Womb, and is at set times purged forth what is superfluous; and it is an excrement of the last nutriment of the fleshy parts, for what is too much for nature's use she casts it forth; for women have soft loose flesh and small heat, and cannot concoct all the blood she provides, nor discuss it but by this way of purgation.

## Book IV, Chap. 1 'Rules for Women that Are Come to Their Labour'

... The same things almost all are proper when the Child is living and comes to be born, but if her Travaill be long, the Midwife must refresh her with some

Chicken's broth or the Yolk of a poached Egg, with a little bread, or some wine, or strong water, but moderately taken, and withal to cheer her up with good words, & stroaking down her belly above her Navel gently with her hand, for that makes the Child move downwards: She must bid her hold in her breath as much as she can, for that will cause more force to bring out the Child.

Take notice that all women do not keep the same posture in their delivery; some lie in their beds, being very weak, some sit in a stool or chair, or rest upon the side of the bed, held by other women that come to the Labour.

If the Woman that lyeth in be very fat, fleshly, or gross, let her lie groveling on the place, for that opens the womb, and thrusts it downwards. The Midwife must annoint her hands with Oil of Lilies, and the Woman's Secrets, or with Oil of Almonds, and so with her hands handle and unloose the parts, and observe how the Child lieth, and stirreth, and so help as time and occasion direct. But above all take heed you force not the birth till the time be come, and the Child come forward and appears ready to come forth.

Now the danger were much to force delivery, because when the woman hath laboured sore, if she rest not a while, she will not be able presently to endure it, her strength being spent before.

Source: Jane Sharp, *The Midwives Book* (1671).

## Document 4

### Thomas/ine Hall

*Thomas (also known as Thomasine) Hall was examined at the General Court in Virginia in 1629 after accusations of lying with a servant and being both male and female.*

*Examinations taken before John Pott Esquire governor the 25th day of March Anno [1629]*

Francis England of the age of twenty years or thereabouts sworn and examined saith that Thomas Hall (being examined by Captain Basse whether he were man or woman as himself did confess to this examinate) told this examinate that he answered Captain Basse that he was both man and woman. And this examinate further saith that the said Hall being at Atkins Arbor one Nicholas [blank] asked him why he went in woman's apparel the said Hall answered in the hearing of this deponent 'I go in woman's apparel to get a bit for my cat'. And he further saith there was a rumour and report that the said Hall did lie with a maid of Mr Richard Bennett's called Great Bess. And he likewise saith that he this examinate and one Roger Rodes being at the upper planation after it had been rumoured that the said Hall was a man and that he was put in man's apparel, the said Hall being then there with them, the said Rodes told Hall 'Thou has been reported to be a woman and now thou art proved to be a man, I will see what thou carriest'. Whereupon the said Rodes laid hands upon the said Hall, and this examinate did so likewise, and they threw the said Hall on his back, and then this examinant felt the said Hall and pulled out his members whereby it appeared that he was a perfect man, and more he cannot depose.

John Atkins of the age of 29 years or thereabouts sworn and examined deposeth and saith That Mr Stacy having reported that Hall now a servant unto this examinate was as he thought a man and woman, not long after, the said Hall (then being servant to Robert Eyres and John Tyos) and being at Nicholas Eyres his house, Alice Long Dorothy Rodes and Barbara Hall being at that time in the said house, upon the said Report did search the said Hall and found (as they then said) that he was a man but the said Tyos swore the said Hall was a woman (as the said Dorothy Rodes did often affirm unto this deponent). Whereupon Captain Basse examined the said Hall in the presence of this deponent whether he were man or woman, the said Hall replied he was both only he had not the use of the man's part [there] was a piece of flesh growing at the _____ [page torn] belly as big as the top of his little finger [an] inch long whereupon Capt. Basse commanded him to be put in woman's apparel, but the aforesaid searchers were not fully resolved, but stood in doubt of what they had formerly affirmed, and being (about the twelfth of February) at this examinate's house the said Hall dwelling them with him, and finding the said Hall asleep did again search him and then also found the said Hall to be a man and at that presently called this examinate to see the proof thereof, but the said Hall seeming to stare as if she had been awake this examinate left him and at that instant could see nothing. But the Sunday following, those searchers being again assembled and the wife of Allen Kinaston and the wife of Ambrose Griffin being in company with them were again desirous to search the said Hall, and having searched him the presence of this deponent did then likewise find him to be a man. Whereupon this examinate asked him if that were all he had to which he answered I have a piece of an hole and thereupon this deponent commanded him to lie on his back and shew the same. And the said women searching him again did again find him to be a man, Whereupon the foresaid examinate did command him to be put into man's apparel. And the day following went to Captain Basse, and told him that the said Hall was found to be a man and desired that he might be punished for his abuse. And this deponent further saith that the said Hall (as this deponent hath heard) did question the said Alice Long for reporting that he had lain with a maid of Mr Richard Bennett's, to which she answered I reported it not but Jonny Tyos his man reported so much. And this is all this examinate can say.

Thomas Hall examined saith that he being born at or near Newcastle upon Tyne was as he hath been often told christened by the name of Thomasine and so was called and went clothed in women's apparel there until the age of 12 years at which age the said Examinant's mother sent him to his Aunt in London and there he lived ten years until Cale's Action, at which time a brother of his being passed for that service this examinate cut off his hair and changed his apparel into the fashion of man and went over as soldier in the Isle of Rée being in the habit of a man, from whence when he was returned he came to Plymouth, and there he changed himself into woman's apparel and made bone lace and did other work with his needle, and shortly after Shipping being ready for a voyage into this country he Changed again his apparel into the habit of a man and so came over into this country.

It was thereupon at this Court ordered that it shall be published in the plantation where the said Hall liveth that he is a man and a woman, that all the inhabitants there may take notice thereof and that he shall go clothed in man's apparel, only his head to be attired in a coif and crosscloth with an apron before him And that he shall find sureties for his good behaviour from Quarter Court to Quarter Court until the Court shall discharge him and Capt. Nathaniel Basse is ordered to see this order executed accordingly.

Source: Library of Congress, Thomas Jefferson Papers, Virginia General Court (1622–9), also published in H. R. McIlwaine (ed.), *Minutes of the Council and General Court of Colonial Virginia, Richmond, VA* (1924).

## Document 5

### Leo Africanus

*The Moroccan traveller Leo Africanus's* Geographical History of Africa *(first published in Venice in 1550; translated into English by John Porty in 1600) introduced European readers to tales of the exotic practices of African culture, repeating suggestions of reversed gender roles that were as old as Herodotus. These descriptions of gender inversions are from the sections on Morocco and Egypt.*

### Of the Inns of Fez

The inn-keepers of Fez being all of one family called Elcheua, go apparelled like women, and shave their beards, and are so delighted to imitate women, that they will not only counterfeit their speech, but will sometimes also sit down and spin. Each one of these hath his concubine, whom he accompanieth as if she were his own lawful wife; albeit the said concubines are not only ill-favoured in countenance, but notorious for their bad life and behaviour.

### Of the Fortune-Tellers and Some Other Artisans in Fez

The third kind of diviners are women-witches, which are affirmed to have familiarity with devils: some devils they call red, some white, and some black devils: and when they will tell any man's fortune, they perfume themselves with certain odours, saying, that then they possess themselves with that devil which they called for: afterward changing their voice, they feign the devil to speak within them: then they which come to enquire, ought with great fear and trembling ask these vile and abominable witches such questions as they mean to propound, and lastly offering some fee unto the devil, they depart. But the wiser and honester sort of people call these women *Sahaoat*, which in Latin signifieth *Fricatrices*, because they have a damnable custom to commit unlawful venery among themselves, which I cannot express in any modester terms. If fair women come unto them at any time, these abominable witches will burn in lust towards them no otherwise than lusty younkers do towards young maids, and will in the devil's behalf demand for a reward, that they may lie with them: and so by this means it often falleth out, that thinking thereby to fulfil the devil's command they lie with the witches. Yea some there are, which being allured with the delight of this abominable vice, will desire the company of these witches, and feigning themselves to be sick, will either call one of the witches home to them, or will send their husbands for the same purpose: and so the witches perceiving how the matter stands, will say that the woman is possessed with a devil, and that she can no way be cured, unless she be admitted into their society. With these words her silly husband being persuaded, doth not only permit her so to do, but makes also a sumptuous banquet unto the damned crew of witches: which being done, they use to dance very strangely at the noise of drums: and so the poor man commits his false wife to their filthy disposition. Howbeit some there are that will soon conjure the devil with a good cudgel out of their wives: others feigning themselves to be possessed with a devil, will deceive the said witches, as their wives have been deceived by them.

## [Cairo]

The women go costly attired, adorning their foreheads and necks with frontlets and chains of pearl, and on their heads they wear a sharp and slender bonnet of a span high, being very precious and rich. Gowns they wear of woollen cloth with straight sleeves, being curiously embroidered with needlework, over which they cast certain veils of most excellent fine cloth of India. They cover their heads and faces with a kind of black scarf, through which beholding others, they cannot be seen themselves. Upon their feet they wear fine shoes and pantoffles, somewhat after the Turkish fashion. These women are so ambitious and proud, that all of them disdain either to spin or to play the cooks: wherefore their husbands are constrained to buy victuals ready dressed at the cooks' shops: for very few, except such as have a great family, use to prepare and dress their victuals in their own houses. Also they vouchsafe great liberty unto their wives: for the good man being gone to the tavern or victualling-house, his wife tricking up her self in costly apparel, and being perfumed with sweet and precious odours, walketh about the city to solace her self, and parley with her kinsfolks and friends. They use to ride upon asses more than horses, which are broke to such a gentle pace, that they go easier than any ambling horse. These asses they cover with most costly furniture, and let them out unto women to ride upon, together with a boy to lead the ass, and certain footmen to run by … The citizens in their common talk use ribald and filthy speeches: and (that I may pass over the rest in silence) it falleth out oftentimes that the wife will complain of her husband unto the judge, that he doth not his duty nor contenteth her sufficiently in the night season, whereupon (as it is permitted by the Mahometan law) the women are divorced and married unto other husbands.

Source: Leo Africanus, *A Geographical Historie of Africa... Gathered Partly out of his Owne Diligent Observations, and Partly out of the Ancient Records and Chronicles of the Arabians and Mores...*, trans. John Pory (1600), pp. 130–31; 148–9; 314–15.

## Document 6

### Dinah, 'a Black'

*Dinah, a Bristol servant, was set to be transported by her mistress, but persuaded the Mayor's Court to free her to stay and work. Such forcible transportations were illegal but in Dinah's case were complicated by her being Black and probably, previously enslaved. Her baptism gave some protection, as did the witnesses who came to support her. 'Get a being' probably means 'get a living'.*

The fifth of July 1667

Whereas one Dinah a Black hath lived as a servant to one Dorothy Smith within this City for the space of five years last past and since hath received Christian Baptism still desiring so to live here under the preaching of the Gospel and her said Mistress having secretly and against her will caused her to be conveyed aboard the ship Robert to be transported to some foreign plantations; Complaint whereof having been made to us and upon examination the truth of the premises appearing to us and her said mistress now refusing to take her into her service till the next General Sessions till this cause shall be there fully heard and determined. It is ordered that the said Dinah shall be at liberty to remain where she can get a being till those Sessions. And further that the said Mistress and Dinah do both then appear with their proof and witnesses on both sides.

Thomas Langston, Mayor
Walter Sandy
John Knight
1667

Source: Bristol Record Office, Mayor and Aldermen's Committee: Orders of Mayor and Aldermen (1666–1673), BA: M/BCC/MAY/1/3.

## Document 7

### Runaway

*In the last half of the seventeenth century the London Gazette newspaper regularly featured advertisements such as this, often employing mediators like Bartholomew Gracedieu.*

A Negro Woman, short but thick, about Twenty years of age, with a Stuff Jacket buttoned down before, a Stuff Petticoat, black Shoes, and sad coloured stockings, with holes in her Ears for Rings, a Cap with a blue Ribbon on her head, marked with a P and a B on her back; Run away from her Mistress on Friday night the Fourth Instant: If any one can give tidings to Mr Bartholomew Gracedieu at the Flying Horse in Thames-Street nigh the Bridge, of the said Negro, so that she may be delivered to her Mistress again, shall have 40s. reward.

Source: *The London Gazette* no. 1946 (10–14 July 1684).

## Document 8

*Katherine Austen*

*Katherine Austen was born into a London draper's family in 1629, and was married and widowed by the age of thirty. During her widowhood she composed a manuscript book of poems, reflections and advice to her children: this piece, written in the 1660s, is addressed to her son Thomas who, as his father had been, was enrolled at an Oxford college.*

To my Son Thomas Austen

A fellow of a College is made up of pride and unmannerliness (in diverse of them). And they that are fellow commoners, learn those ill habits. I repent me of nothing more I made you one. I had better have took the good counsel of Dr Wilbe not for the charges, as the diverse dangers is in it. What makes noble men to be so extremely civil but being used from all men to receive a great respect by observance and keeping their hats off in their presence. Which does not exclude them theirs by their dignity above others. But civility and good breeding obliges the same answerable return. As the Lord Manchester to Cousin T.K. put off his hat all the time he had business to my Lord. And truly in my estimation this very rude fashion creates abundance of pride in Colleges. Either all lordly. Nay Kingly. Or else vassals, and lavish in the royalty of Colleges.

And certainly for the ill breeding and unaccomplishments in colleges, enforces Gentlemen of quality to send their sons to travel to learn civility and sweetness of deportment, for by the early habit of pride, and surliness and stoutness of carriage they hardly ever forget it while they live....

Whatever the fashion is I would have your demeanour other ways. And though you may go scot free, hat free, be not so rude in your carriage but if a beggar put off his hat, give the like.

Source: British Library Add. Mss. 4454, f. 40, also published in Sarah Ross (ed.), *Katherine Austen's Book M* (Tempe, AZ: Arizona Center for Medieval and Renaissance Studies, 2011).

## Document 9

*Frank North*

*Anne North took her grandchildren to live with her in Suffolk when her son Francis North, Lord Chief Justice, was widowed in 1678. She was about sixty-five and had herself been widowed the previous year. These letters to the children's father record the progress of her grandson Frank into breeches. The end of the second letter refers to a disagreement between herself and her eldest son over her right to present to the local church.*

For the Rt Honourable the Lord Chief Justice at his house in Chancery Lane. These.

[Tostock] 10 October, '79

Dear Son,

Nobody believed that you could make so short a stay here, so that the letters are directed hither still, and this enclosed was brought me yesterday. You cannot believe the great concern that was in the whole family here last Wednesday, it being the day that the tailor was to help to dress little Frank in his breeches in order to the making an everyday suit by it. Never had any bride that was to be dressed upon her wedding night more hands about her, some the legs and some the arms, the tailor buttoning and others putting on the sword, and so many lookers on that had I not had a finger amongst them I could not have seen him. When he was quite dressed he acted his part as well as any of them, for he desired he might go down to inquire for the little gentleman that was there the day before in a black coat, and speak to the men to tell the gentleman when he came from school that here was a gallant with very fine clothes and a sword to have waited upon him and would come again upon Sunday next. But this was not all, for there was great contriving while he was dressing who should have the first salute, but he said if old Lane had been here she should, but he gave it me to quiet them all. They are very fit, everything, and he looks taller and prettier than in his coats. Little Charles rejoiced as much as he did, for he jumped all the while about him and took notice of everything. I went to Bury and bought everything for another suit, which will be finished upon Saturday, so the coats are to be quite left off upon Sunday. I consider it is not yet term time and since you could not have the pleasure of the first sight I have resolved you should have a full relation from

Your most affectionate Mother,

A. North.

When he was dressed he asked Buckle whether muffs were out of fashion because they had not sent him one.

For [as above]

[Tostock] 12 October, '79

Dear Son,

I thank you for sending me so particular an account of the little ones' ages, which I think as forward children for these times as can be. I gave you an account in my last that this day was designed wholly to throw off the coats and write man, and great good fortune it was to have it a fair day. It was carried with a great deal of privacy purposely to surprise Mr. Camborne, and it took so well as to put him to the blush as soon as he saw him in the church, which pleased Frank not a little. I perceive it proves as I thought, that your brother North would think I infringed upon his right when I presented to Drinkston. But I wonder he should declare so much when he knows it is my unquestionable due: it looks as if he grudged at what I have, though it be but the honour and gratifying of another, without any profit to myself, and indeed I cannot take it well of him for he lays an aspersion both upon my dear Lord and myself, but I shall look upon it only as selfishness and let him say his pleasure ...

Source: Roger North, *The Autobiography of the Hon. Roger North*, ed. Augustus Jessopp (D. Nutt, 1887), pp. 215–17.

## Document 10

### Mawdlin Gawen

*Mawdlin Gawen appeared at London's Bridewell in 1575 on the charge of wearing men's clothes.*

Mawdlin Gawen sent in by my Lord Mayor and the aldermen his brethren for going and putting herself into man's apparel she being of the age of 22 years or thereabouts born in the parish of Thame in Oxfordshire. Saith that she was in service with one Goodwife Oliver in the said town of Thame an innkeeper where she dwelled two years. And from thence she said she went to Teddington in Bedfordshire to an uncle of hers to which place she came on Monday in Whitsun week last. And by her said uncle was placed with one Mr Chaunce the Lord Chenye's Steward. And there remained until Michaelmas last. And then came to one Smith a tanner dwelling in Teddington aforesaid and was hired with him for one year.

And that she then by the enticement of one Thomas Ashwell also servant with the said Smith did consent to roam from her said master with the same Thomas, and so they two came from thence to Stansted in Hertfordshire where they tarried three days. And from thence they came to London to one Thomas Balle's house in Finche Lane, the said Thomas Ashwell by the way always said she was his kinswoman. And being in Finche Lane she was brought to one Mr Fluett where she was placed in service, the said Ashwell coming to her to the said Mr Fluett's house. The said Mr Fluett asking, what countrywoman she was she said she was born in Collyweston which the said Ashwell also affirmed. And in asking them how far it was from Stansted because the truth might be known, the said Ashwell could not tell. Nevertheless the said Fluett received her into service where she remained about three weeks. But the said Gawen saith she spake not with the said Ashwell from the time she was there placed in service until Thursday last, at which time he persuaded her to meet him at Paul's Wharf the Tuesday next following in the morning by four of the clock. She answered him again she would not come in her own apparel. And he told her, that what apparel soever she came in he would receive her and put on her own.

And the time appointed she changed her self into man's apparel which she had in her said mistress's house being about two of the clock after midnight and came away and so came to Paul's Wharf being the place appointed but the said Ashwell was not there present nor came not according to his appointment, she calling there for a boat to go down westward a waterman looking out of a window said it was too early and she said she would stay until it were time and that he would go. Whereupon the waterman came down and opened his door and she went in to his house with her farthingale under her arm which she cast down upon the ground within the door. And then she desired the waterman himself to do so much as to poll her and she said she would give him a **groat** for his labour. And the waterman made her believe he would so do but he sent his man for the constable when he perceived what she was and so made a strife saying he lacked his scissors and so made as though he sent his man for them as he told her, and his man tarrying long went himself for the constable, and when the constable came she was apprehended and she saith she told the constable that she dwelled in Philpott Lane with one Goodwife Osborne.

Also she saith that the said Thomas Ashwell began to live wickedly with her from Shrovetide last until such time as she was placed in service here in London. And that he had the use of her body carnally divers and sundry times as at Stansted aforesaid and other places more for the which wickedness she had by order of the Lord Mayor and the bench correction.

Source: London Metropolitan Archives, Bridewell Court Book II, fos 114v–115v (20 April 1575), microfilm, available online at www. archives.museumofthemind.org.

## Document 11

### Hic Mulier

*The anonymous short pamphlet attacking the cross-gendered fashions of early seventeenth-century London uses a masculine article (hic, meaning this) for a feminine noun (mulier, meaning woman).*

Come, then, you masculine women, for you are my subject, you that have made admiration an ass and fooled him with a deformity never before dreamed of; that have made yourselves stranger things than ever Noah's Ark unloaded or Nile engendered, whom to name, he that named all things might study an age to give you a right attribute; whose like are not found in any antiquary's study, in any seaman's travel, nor in any painter's cunning. You that are stranger than strangeness itself; whom wise men wonder at, boys shout at, and goblins themselves start at; you that are the gilt dirt which embroiders playhouses, the painted statues which adorn caroches, and the perfumed carrion that bad men feed on in brothels: 'tis of you I entreat and of your monstrous deformity. You that have made your bodies like antique boscage or crotesco work, not half man/half woman, half fish/half flesh, half beast/half monster, but all odious, all devil; that have cast off the ornaments of your sexes to put on the garments of shame; that have laid by the bashfulness of your natures to gather the impudence of harlots, that have buried silence to revive slander; that are all things but that which you should be, and nothing less than friends to virtue and goodness; that have made the foundation of your highest detested work from the lowest despised creatures that record can give testimony of: the one cut from the commonwealth at the gallows; the other is well known. From the first you got the false armoury of yellow starch (for to wear yellow on white or white upon yellow is by the rules of heraldry baseness, bastardy, and indignity), the folly of imitation, the deceitfulness of flattery, and the grossest baseness of all baseness, to do whatever a greater power will command you. From the other you have taken the monstrousness of your deformity in apparel, exchanging the modest attire of the comely hood, cowl, coif, handsome dress or kerchief, to the cloudy ruffianly broad-brimmed hat and wanton feather; the modest upper parts of a concealing straight gown, to the loose, lascivious civil embracement of a French doublet being all unbuttoned to entice, all of one shape to hide deformity, and extreme short waisted to give a most easy way to every luxurious action; the glory of a fair large hair, to the shame of most ruffianly short locks; the side, thick gathered, and close guarding safeguards to the short, weak, thin, loose, and every hand-entertaining short bases; for needles, swords; for prayerbooks, bawdy legs; for modest gestures, giantlike behaviours; and for women's modesty, all mimic and apish incivility. These are your founders, from these you took your copies, and, without amendment, with these you shall come to perdition.

Source: *Hic Mulier: or, The Man-Woman: Being a Medicine to Cure the Coltish Disease of the Staggers in the Masculine-Feminines of our Times* (1620), sig. A3v–B1.

## Document 12

### A Joke

*Sir Nicholas L'Estrange, a Norfolk baronet, kept a book of his favourite jests, with attributions for each; this one was his mother's joke.*

A plain country fellow, following his daughter to church to be married: well go thy ways says he, for there goes as pure a virgin as ever man laid leg over; but at dinner in all the mirth and jollity, our bride grew quamish in her stomach, and (striving to smother her disease) swooned away for a goose rump; and within few weeks after, this pure virgin was delivered of a most goodly knave-child [My Mother].

Source: Nicholas L'Estrange, *'Merry Passages and Jeasts': A Manuscript Jestbook of Sir Nicholas Le Strange, 1603–1655* (Salzburg: University of Salzburg, 1974), p. 105.

## Document 13

### *Edward Lacy and Elizabeth Inkberrow*

*Edward Lacy, a married man, and Elizabeth Inkberrow, a widow, were bound over to behave by their neighbours in Riple, Worcestershire, in 1661; the names beside each article are those who made the complaints.*

*Worcester County*

**Articles of the Good Behaviour exhibited September 6 1661 against Edward Lacy of Riple labourer and Elizabeth Inkberrow of the same parish widow before Henry Bromley esquire Justice of the Peace**

| | |
|---|---|
| Isabell Morris jun.<br>Thomas Clarke jun. | 1. That the said Edward Lacy did threaten to go away from his wife and leave her nothing but a bed and the rags on her back as he himself expressed, whereby she may become a charge to the parish. |
| Robert Tustian<br>Thomas Best jun.<br>William Morris | 2. That he the said Lacy will not cohabit with his wife, but hath lain for the most part of twenty weeks last past at the widow Inkberrow's house giving a great cause of scandal and offence to the neighbourhood, who generally suspect that they live together in incontinency. |
| Margaret Fairelock | 3. That besides the general fame the said Lacy hath been seen in the bed with the said widow Inkberrow, and hath been heard to wish his knife in his heart if he lay with his wife again. |
| Anne Land | 4. That the said Lacy when a difference happened betwixt the said widow Inkberrow and her mother, did provoke and encourage her to offer abuse and violence to her said mother. |

The Articles against the aforesaid Elizabeth Inkberrow widow are

| | |
|---|---|
| Anne Land | 1. That upon a difference betwixt her mother and her self the said Elizabeth Inkberrow did assault hurt and abuse her said Mother. |

| | |
|---|---|
| Robert Tustian<br>Thomas Best | 2. That the said Elizabeth Inkberrow by her lewd carriage doth give great offence to the neighbourhood and a general cause of suspicion that she lived in whoredom with the aforesaid Lacy, having entertained him at her house almost this half year last past, and lodging him there from his wife though his own house is very near adjoining to hers: whereby his affection is alienated from his wife, which hath been a great cause of sadness and affliction to her. |
| Margaret Fairelock | 3. That besides the general suspicion it is known that she hath gone to bed to the said Lacy, having been seen in his bed with him. |
| Robert Tustian | 4. That she is much suspected to be with child, and that there is great suspicion and fear that she hath a design to destroy her child there having been savin found in her bed, and she having been known to have tampered with those that pretend to give physic. |

Source: Worcestershire Record Office, QS 98/37.

## Document 14

### *Leonard Wheatcroft*

*Leonard Wheatcroft (1627–1707), a Derbyshire tailor and parish clerk, kept a manuscript notebook with a narrative of his courtship of his wife, Elizabeth. This extract is from one of the earliest entries, where a journey from London brings him to the parish festival at Ashover known as the wakes.*

And I being present at that wakes, I had some intelligence of a young maid that would be there by one of her relations, who told me she was very fortunate, besides beautiful lovely.

So in process of time she came, and many more with her, both relations and friends, and being all drawn up into a garden, where was a famous arbour which at that time held 28 people, amongst whom was placed this beautiful damsel. Then after I had saluted several of my friends and acquaintance, I drew a little nearer this young lady, whom I had never seen before. So after we had parled awhile and could not agree we parted and she returned to her castle again; from which hold she sent me a challenge, and withal hang her flag of defiance against me; which I no sooner perceiving all this, I mustered up all my man forces, and close siege to her, which siege lasted for the space 23 months and more, before she would yield I should enter, etc. But what happened in this long and tedious siege was as followeth.

After I had enclosed her in her castle called by the name of Winster (not far from Bakewell in the Peak) we had several parleys, but in many of them we could not agree, and she like a courageous commander always cheered up her resolved and commanded thoughts to resist poor me. But being as then a never-daunted soldier in the wars of Mars, I played several cannon-like letters against the main tower of her heart, and every day laying closer siege than other, as you shall hear hereafter.

Source: *The Courtship Narrative of Leonard Wheatcroft, Derbyshire Yeoman*, ed. George Parfitt and Ralph Houlbrooke (Reading: Whiteknights Press, 1986), pp. 41–2.

## Document 15

### Elizabeth Browne

*Questioned for illegitimacy and to discover the name of her child's father at the Somerset Quarter Sessions in 1607.*

The Examination of Elizabeth Browne of Wisterton spinster ... 10 August 1607

She saith that she was the Saturday before St Luketide last retained into the service of one John Norris of Wisterton and within one month next after her retaining the said Norris service, one William Norris dwelling at home with his father made love to this examinant and had to do with her in his father's hall floor in the night time when his father was abed, and about sevenight after the said William Norris being on his father's mow, caused this examinant to come up to throw sheaves to him, at which time the said William Norris had to do with her again and from that time forth, he had his pleasure of her, sometimes when she was making the beds and sometime elsewhere, as often as pleased him.

Source: Somerset Archives, Q/SR 2/12.

## Document 16

### The Country Justice

*Michael Dalton's book was a guide for magistrates; these sections cover bastardy and the felony of rape.*

### Chapter 2 'Bastardy'

Every Justice of Peace, upon his discretion, may (as it seemeth) bind to the good behaviour, him that is charged, or suspected to have begotten a bastard child, to the end that he may be forthcoming when the child shall be borne; otherwise there will be no putative father, when the two justices (after the birth of the child) shall come to take order according to the Statute of 18 Eliz. c. 3. The like may be done after the birth of the child, and before such order taken....

Also it seemeth the mother may be examined upon oath, concerning the reputed father, and of the time, and other circumstances, for that in this case the matter and the trial thereof dependeth chiefly upon the examination and testimony of the mother...

By the Statute 7. Jac. it appeareth that the Justices of the peace shall now commit such lewd women to the house of correction, there to be punished, etc. And therefore it seemeth that the Justices of Peace may not punish (by corporal punishment) the mother by force of this Statute of 18 Eliz. 3 and then to send them to the house of correction ...

But such corporal punishment, or commitment to the house of correction, is not to be until after that the woman is delivered of her child, neither are the Justices of Peace to meddle with the woman until that the child be born (and she strong again) lest the woman being weak, or the child wherewith she is, happen to miscarry; for you shall find that about 31. Eliz. a woman great with child, and suspected for incontinency, was commanded (by the Master of Bridewell in London) to be whipped there, by reason whereof she travailed, and was delivered of her child before her time, etc. And for this the said masters of Bridewell were in the Star-Chamber fined to the Queen at a great sum, and were further ordered to pay a sum of money to the said woman ...

Every lewd woman which shall have a bastard, which may be chargeable to the parish, the justices of peace shall commit such woman unto the house of correction, there to be punished and set on work for one year: and if she shall eftsoons offend again; then to be committed to the house of correction, as aforesaid; and there to remain until she can put in good sureties for her good behaviour, not to offend again ...

It seemeth also (by the words of this statute 7. *Jacobi*) that such a woman shall not be sent to the house of correction, until after the child be born, and that it be living; for it must be such a child as may be chargeable to the parish.

Also it seemeth that such a bastard child, is not to be sent with the mother to the house of correction, but rather that the child should remain in the town where it was born (or settled with the mother) and there to be relieved by the work of the mother, or by relief from the reputed father... and yet the common opinion and practice is otherwise, *sc.* to send the child, with the mother, to the house of correction; And this may also seem reasonable, where the child sucketh on the mother ...

## Chapter 107 'Felonies by Statute'

Women, *sc.* to ravish a woman where she doth neither consent before nor after, or to ravish any woman with force, though she do consent after, it is felony: and the offender shall have no benefit of clergy ...

Now Ravishment is here taken in one and the same signification with Rape, which is a violent deflowering of a woman, or a carnal knowledge had of the body of a woman against her will ...

A woman that is ravished, ought presently to levy open hue and cry, or to complain thereof presently to some credible persons as it seemeth ...

If a woman at the time of the supposed rape, do conceive with child, by the ravisher, this is no rape, for a woman cannot conceive with child, except she do consent ...

And yet if a man ravish a woman, who consenteth for fear of death or duress, this is ravishment against her will, for that consent ought to be voluntary and free.

> Source: Michael Dalton, *The Countrey Justice, Containing the Practice of the Justices of the Peace out of their Sessions* (1635), pp. 37–9, 281.

## Document 17

### James I and George Villiers

*James I's letters to Villiers, Duke of Buckingham, described a love widely assumed to be sexual in the terms of family relations; Buckingham wrote to him as 'Dear dad and gossip'.*

[December 1623?]

My only sweet and dear child,

Notwithstanding of your desiring me not to write yesterday, yet had I written in the evening if, at my coming out of the park, such a drowsiness had not come upon me as I was forced to set and sleep in my chair half an hour. And yet I cannot content myself without sending you this present, praying God that I may have a joyful and comfortable meeting with you and that we may make at this Christmas a new marriage ever to be kept hereafter; for, God so love me, as I desire only to live in this world for your sake, and that I had rather live banished in any part of the earth with you than live a sorrowful widow's life without you. And so God bless you, my sweet child and wife, and grant that ye may ever be a comfort to your dear dad and husband.

James R.

> Source: *Letters of King James VI and I*, ed. G. P. V. Akrigg (Berkeley, CA: University of California Press, 1984), p. 431.

## Document 18

### Samuel Pepys

*At a dinner to celebrate the birth of his friends' child, Pepys asked the gossips' advice about his apparent infertility.*

26 July 1664.

All the morning at the office. At noon to Anth. Joyce's to our gossips' dinner; I had sent a dozen and a half of bottles of wine thither and paid my double share besides, which is 18 s. Very merry we were, and when the women were merry and ris from table, I above with them, ne'er a man but I; I begin discourse of my not getting with children and prayed them to give me their opinions and advice; and they freely and merrily did give me these ten among them. 1. Do not hug my wife too hard nor too much. 2. Eat no late suppers. 3. Drink juice of sage. 4. Tent and toast. 5. Wear cool Holland-drawers. 6. Keep stomach warm and back cool. 7. Upon my query whether it was best to do at night or morn, they answered me neither one nor another, but when we have most mind to it. 8. Wife not to go too straight-laced. 9. Myself to drink Mum and sugar. 10. Mrs Ward did give me to change my plate. The 3$^{rd}$, 4$^{th}$, 6$^{th}$, 7$^{th}$ and 10$^{th}$ they all did seriously declare and lay much stress upon them, as rules fit to be observed indeed, and especially the last: to lie with our heads where our heels do, or at least to make the bed high at feet and low at head.

Source: *The Diary of Samuel Pepys*, vol. v (1664), ed. Robert Latham and William Matthews (London: HarperCollins, 1995), p. 222.

## Document 19

### Aristotle's Masterpiece

Aristotle's Masterpiece, *a pseudo-Aristotelian popular guide to sex and reproduction, was reprinted in various editions from the late seventeenth century into the twentieth. Its summary of beliefs about 'the secrets of generation' combined ancient learning and popular knowledge. This discussion of the question of parental resemblance also stresses the alignment of femininity with the left-hand side and masculinity with the right, a fundamental principle of pre-modern gender relations.*

*Chap. III 'The reason why children are often like their parents, and what the mother's imagination contributes thereto: how the mother contributes seed, and is a companion in the whole generation; and whence grows the kind, viz. whether the man or the woman is the cause of the male or female child, etc.'*

It is the opinion of learned physicians, grounded upon reason, that if a woman in the act of copulation afford most seed, her likeness will have the greatest impression upon the child; but if on the contrary, then will follow the contrary effects; or if a proportionable quantity proceed from either, then will the similitude depend upon either.

*Lactantius* is of opinion, that when a man's seed falls on the left side of the womb a male child may be gotten: but by reason it is the proper place for a female, there will be something in it greatly resembling a woman, viz, it will be fairer, whiter, and smoother, not very subject to have hair on the body or chin, long lank hair on the head, the voice small and sharp, and the courage feeble; and arguing yet further, he says, that a female may perchance be procreated if the seed fall on the right side; but then through extraordinary heat, she will be very large boned, full of courage, endued with a big voice, and have her chin and bosom hairy, not being so clear as others of the sex; subject to quarrel with her husband when married, for the superiority, etc. Yet in case of the similitude, nothing is more powerful than the imagination of the mother; for if she conceive in her mind, or do by chance fasten her eyes upon any object, and imprint it in her memory, the child in its outward parts frequently has some representation thereof; so whilst a man and woman are in the act of copulation, if the woman earnestly behold his countenance and fix her mind thereon, without all peradventure, the child will resemble the father; nay so powerful is its operation, that though a woman be in unlawful copulation, yet if fear or any thing else causes her to fix her mind upon her husband, the child will resemble him, though he never got it. The same effect, according to the opinion of the learned, proceeds from imagination in cause of warts, mouldspots, stains, dashes, and the figures of strange things, though indeed they sometimes happen thro' frights and extravagant longings. Many women there are, that seeing a hare cross them when great with child, will, through the strength of imagination, bring forth a child with a hairy-lip. Some children again are born with flat noses, wry mouths, great blubber lips, and ill shaped bodies, and most ascribe the reason to the strange conceit of the mother, who has busied her eyes and mind upon some ill shaped or distorted creature; therefore it greatly behoves all woman with child to avoid any monstrous sight, or at least to have a steadfast mind, not easily fixed upon any one thing more than another.

Source: *Aristoteles Master-piece, or, The Secrets of Generation Displayed in all the Parts Thereof* (1684), pp. 24–6.

# Document 20

## *Ralph Josselin*

*Ralph Josselin kept a diary during the years he was vicar of Earls Colne, Essex from 1641 to 1683. The section below comes from the early part, which was written retrospectively.*

My wife now growing big and ill my mother came from Olney to us upon a Tuesday lecture day April 12 [1642] after sermon having waited upon God in his house, my wife called her women and God was merciful to me in my house giving her a safe deliverance, and a daughter which on Thursday April 21ˢᵗ was baptized by the name of Mary: Mr Rich: Harlakenden: Mr John Litle: Mrs Mary Mildmay and my wife's mother being witnesses. I entertained my neighbours all about it cost me £6 and 13s. 4d. at least: they shewed much love to me from all parts. God blessed my wife to be a nurse, and our child thrived, and was even then a pleasant comfort to us. God wash it from corruption and sanctify it and make it his own. But it pleased God my wives breasts were sore which was a grievance and sad cut to her but with use of means in some distance of time they healed up. This spring times grew fearful in the rising of the year about Midsummer we began to raise private arms: I found a musket for my part and the King was beginning to raise an army. The Parliament did the like ...

1643: In spring now my wife weaned her daughter and began to breed again. God gave us both our health in a greater measure than I had before or my wife of late days ...

August 2: being Wed: I was taken very ill with a quotidian ague I had three fits, the physician told me I would have one harsh one more but on Friday night seeking God for my health that if it pleased him I might still go on in my calling I was strangely persuaded I should have no more fits neither had I: Lord let me never forget thy goodness but let me the Lord because he hath heard my cry answered my request ...

Aug 8: 1644: I have bought a part in a ship it cost me £14.10s. God send me good speed with the same. I have sent my part in a bag of hops to Sunderland. My sister Mary is come under my roof as a servant, but my respect is and shall be towards her as a sister, God might have made me a waiter upon others. Our former maid Lydia Weston having dwelt with me one year and almost three quarters married into our town, the first that married out of my family.

> Source: *The Diary of Ralph Josselin 1616–1683*, ed. Alan McFarlane
> (Oxford: Oxford University Press, 1976), pp. 12–15.

## Document 21

### Sarah Jinner

*Sarah Jinner, a London woman who described herself as 'student in astrology', published annual almanacs (perhaps the most widely used form of cheap print) for several years in the 1650s and 1660s. Her remedies, many of which dealt with reproductive health, were followed by a calendar of useful dates.*

### Common Syrups which remove Obstruction of the Terms are

Syrup of Mugwort, of Maidenhair, of Chicory with Rhubarb, and the syrup of the five roots; these you may have ready at the Apothecary's.

### Another to move the Terms

Take Mints, Balm, Penny-royal, Marjoram and Southernwood, of each an handful: Aniseeds, Fennel and Caraway seeds, of each an ounce; Polipody, an ounce and an half; Chicory roots, an ounce; cut the roots and herbs very small, and boil them all together in a quart of water till a third part be consumed; then strain it, and sweeten it with Sugar to your own liking, and take thereof as you please.

...

### A Confection to cause Fruitfulness in Man or Woman

Take Rapes, Ivory Shaven, Ashkeys, Cicely, Behen red and white, of each one dram: Cinnamon, Downicum, Mace, Cloves, Galangal, long Pepper, Rosemary flowers, Balsam wood, Blattis, Byzantine Marjoram gentle, Penny royal, of each two scruples: Balm, Bugloss, Citron pieces, of each one scruple: Spica Indie, Amber, Pearls, of each half a scruple: Sugar a pound; decoct the Sugar in Malmsey, and the other things; and make them into a Confection, use of it a little at a time.

...

### A Plaster to remedy the corrupt humours

Take Roses, Cypress Nuts, burnt Ivory, Sandarac, of each one dram, Rosin 2 ounces: boil the Rosin in red Vinegar, till the vinegar be consumed, then mix the other things with it, and make two plasters of it, and apply one to the back, and the other to the womb.

### Another excellent good Plaster to strengthen Women with Child, that do not use to go out half their times

Take oil of Quinces, oil of Roses, oil of Mints, of each one ounces and a half, Comfrey, Blood-stone, red-coral, Sandarac, Date stones burnt: of each one dram mix it with a sufficient quantity of wax to make a salve thereof: and with this anoint the Kidneys and **Mother**.

...

### February, Astrological Observations

This Month will be Epidemical to many Women with child, and of evil consequence to others, not so far gone with child. Many now breeding, endure almost alike torture to bringing forth. Therefore good women make much of your selves, let your Husbands pay for it. I need not exhort some, there are many worthy of reproof, for making too much of naught. Nay, I may add, of never be good. Public Actions, this Month do produce but little. Something will be in the North, and North-East part of the World: private conspiracies will be hatching, but few take effect, or be brought to light.

### For such as think themselves bewitched, that they cannot do the act of Venery

Take flying Ants, mixed with the Oil of Cider, and anoint the defective Instrument.

*To take away the desire of a Woman to the Act of Venery*

Take of a Red Bull's pizzle, and powder it, and put in Wine or Broth, the quantity of a Crown weight of silver, and she will abhor the desire of lying with a man: this may be a good Medicine for the preventing of young Girls throwing themselves away upon Mad-cap fellows. The same Ingredient given to men, will provoke Venery in them that are dull and impotent.

> Sources: Sarah Jinner, *An Almanack and Prognostication for the year of our Lord 1659* (London, 1659) and Sarah Jinner, *An Almanack and Prognostication for the year of our Lord 1664* (London, 1664).

## Document 22

### Jane Minors

*Jane Minors of Barking was presented to the archdeaconry court of Essex on 29 April 1597 for failing to baptise her child and for misconduct during the service of churching.*

We present Jane the wife of John Minors for keeping her child unbaptised a whole month ...

Also detected, for that she very unwomanlike, came to be churched at the end of the said month, together with her child to be baptised, and feasted at a tavern four or five hours in the forenoon: and in the afternoon came to the church, rather to be seen, than upon any devotion, as it seemed; for whilst the minister was burying a corpse, she went out of the church, unchurched, unto the tavern again. And when she was spoken unto by the clerk to return to church again and to give God thanks after her committal of delivery, she answered it was a ceremony. The which abuses of the said Jane, seeing they are so public and notorious, and the example unpunished, may prove dangerous, we pray that your worship would enjoin, that her satisfaction may be also public; to the content of many of good worth.

> Source: William Hale Hale, *A Series of Precedents and Proceedings in Criminal Causes: Extending from the Year 1475 to 1640, Extracted from the Act-Books of Ecclesiastical Courts in the Diocese of London* (F. and J. Rivington, 1847), p. 216.

## Document 23

### Bathsua Makin

*Bathsua Makin, née Reginald (c.1600–after 1675) published her first work, a book of poetry, at 16, and married at 21. Educated by her father, a school-master, she became tutor to Charles I's daughter Princess Elizabeth, and was kept in custody with her in the 1640s. This essay published in 1673 proposed a revival of gentlewomen's education, stressing its utility in protecting religion, and set out the prospectus of her own school.*

### If any desire distinctly to know what they should be instructed in?

I answer, I cannot tell where to begin to admit women, nor from what part of learning to exclude them, in regard of their capacities. The whole encyclopaedia of learning may be useful some way or other to them. Respect indeed is to be had to the nature and dignity of each art and science, as they are more or less subservient to religion, and may be useful to them in their station. I would not deny them the knowledge of Grammar and Rhetoric, because they dispose to speak handsomely. Logic must be allowed, because it is the key to all sciences. Physic, especially visible, as herbs, plants, shrubs, drugs, etc must be studied, because this will exceedingly please themselves, and fit them to be helpful to others. The tongues ought to be studied, especially the Greek and Hebrew, these will enable to the better understanding of the scriptures.

The Mathematics, more especially Geography, will be useful: this puts life into History. Music, Painting, Poetry, etc are a great ornament and pleasure. Some things that are more practical, are not so material, because public employments in the field and courts, are usually denied to women: Yet some have not been inferior to many men even in these things also. Witness Semiramis among the Babylonians; The Queen of Sheba in Arabia; Miriam and Deborah among the Israelites; Catherine de Medici in France; Queen Elizabeth in England ...

In these late times there are several instances of women, when their husbands were serving their King and country, defended their houses, and did all things, as soldiers, with prudence and valour, like men.

They appeared before committees, and pleaded their own causes with good success.

This kind of education will be very useful to women ...

This will be a hedge against heresies. Men are furnished with arts and tongues for this purpose, that they may stop the mouths of their adversaries. And women ought to be learned, that they may stop their ears against seducers. It cannot be imagined so many persons of quality would be so easily carried aside with every wind of doctrine, had they been furnished with these defensive arms; I mean, had they been instructed in the plain rules of artificial reasoning, so as to distinguish a true and forcible argument, from a vain and captious fallacy ...

### Postscript

If any enquire where this education may be performed, such may be informed, That a school is lately erected for gentlewomen at Tottenham High Cross, within four miles of London, in the road to Ware; where Mrs Makin is Governess, who was sometimes tutoress to the Princess Elisabeth, daughter to King

Charles the First; Where, by the blessing of God, gentlewomen may be instructed in the principles of religion, and in all manner of sober and virtuous education: more particularly, in all things ordinarily taught in other schools: as works of all sorts, dancing, music, singing, writing, keeping accounts. Half the time to be spent in these things. The other half to be employed in gaining the Latin and French Tongues: and those that please, may learn Greek and Hebrew, the Italian and Spanish: in all which this Gentlewoman hath a competent knowledge ...

Those that please, may learn Limning, Preserving, Pastry and Cookery.

Those that will allow longer time, may attain some general knowledge in Astronomy, Geography; but especially in Arithmetic and History.

Those that think one language enough for a woman, may forbear the languages, and learn only Experimental Philosophy; and more, or fewer, of the other things aforementioned, as they incline.

> Source: Bathsua Makin, *An Essay to Revive the Ancient Education of Gentlewomen in Religion, Manners, Arts and Tongues with an Answer to the Objections against this Way of Education* (1673), pp. 24–5, 42–3.

## Document 24

### Judith Drake

*Judith Drake (1670–1723) was an author and medical practitioner, married to a physician, and part of an intellectual circle which included Mary Astell. Her* Essay in Defence of the Female Sex, *published anonymously in 1696, was a defence of the virtues of female sociability and conversation; like Astell, her feminist arguments were also part of Tory Anglicanism, seeking to reform moral corruption. Her work, written as a letter to a friend, draws on John Locke's* Essay concerning Human Understanding *to mount a rationalist proof of intellectual equality.*

If Women are not qualified for the Conversation of ingenious Men, or, to get yet further, their friendship, it must be because they want some one condition, or more, necessarily requisite to either. The necessary Conditions of these are sense, and good nature, to which must be added, for Friendship, Fidelity and Integrity. Now if any of these be wanting to our Sex, it must be either because Nature has not been so liberal as to bestow 'em upon us; or because due care has not been taken to cultivate those Gifts to a competent measure in us ...

To proceed therefore if we be naturally defective, the Defect must be either in Soul or Body. In the Soul it can't be, if what I have heard some learned Men maintain, be true, that all Souls are equal, and alike, and that consequently there is no such distinction, as Male and Female Souls; that there are no innate Idea's, but that all the Notions we have, are deriv'd from our External Senses, either immediately, or by Reflection. These Metaphysical Speculations, I must own, Madam, require much more Learning and a stronger Head, than I can pretend to be Mistress of, to be considered as they ought; Yet so bold I may be, as to undertake the defence of these Opinions, when any of our jingling Opponents think fit to refute 'em.

Neither can it be in the Body, (if I may credit the Report of learned Physicians) for there is no difference in the Organization of those Parts, which have any relation to, or influence over the Minds; but the Brain, and all other Parts (which I am not Anatomist enough to name) are contriv'd as well for the plentiful conveyance of Spirits, which are held to be the immediate Instruments of Sensation, in Women, as Men. I see therefore no natural Impediment in the structure of our Bodies; nor does Experience, or Observation argue any: We use all our Natural Faculties, as well as Men, nay, and our Rational too, deducting only for the advantages before mention'd.

Let us appeal yet further to Experience, and observe those Creatures that deviate least from simple Nature, and see if we can find any difference in Sense, or understanding between Males and Females. In these we may see Nature plainest, who lie under no constraint of Custom or Laws, but those of Passion or Appetite, which are Natures, and know no difference of Education, nor receive any Bias by prejudice. We see great distance in Degrees of Understanding, Wit, Cunning and Docility (call them what you please) between the several Species of Brutes. An Ape, a Dog, a Fox, are by daily Observation found to be more Docile, and more Subtle than an Ox, a Swine, or a Sheep. But a She Ape is as full of, and as ready at Imitation as a He; a Bitch will learn as many Tricks in as short a time as a Dog, a Female Fox has as many Wiles as a Male. A thousand instances of this kind might be produc'd; but I think these are so plain, that to instance more were a superfluous labour; I shall only once more take notice, that in Brutes and other Animals there is no difference betwixt Male and Female in point of Sagacity, notwithstanding there is the same distinction of Sexes, that is between Men and Women ...

But if an Argument from Brutes and other Animals shall not be allow'd as conclusive, (though I can't see, why such an Inference should not be valid, since the parity of Reason is the same on both sides in this Case) I shall desire those that hold against us to observe the Country People, I mean the inferior sort of them, such as not having Stocks to follow Husbandry upon their own Score, subsist upon their daily Labour. For amongst these, though not so equal as that of Brutes, yet the Condition of the two Sexes is more level, than amongst Gentlemen, City Traders, or rich Yeomen. Examine them in their several Businesses, and their Capacities will appear equal; but talk to them of things indifferent, and out of the Road of their constant Employment, and the Balance will fall on our side, the Women will be found the more ready and polite. Let us look a little further, and view our Sex in a state of more improvement, amongst our Neighbours the Dutch. There we shall find them managing not only the Domestic Affairs of the Family, but making, and receiving all Payments as well great as small, keeping the Books, balancing the Accounts, and doing all the Business, even the nicest of Merchants, with as much Dexterity and Exactness as their, or our Men can do. And I have often heard some of our considerable Merchants blame the conduct of our Country-Men in this point; that they breed our Women so ignorant of Business; whereas were they taught Arithmetic, and other Arts which require not much bodily strength, they might supply the places of abundance of lusty Men now employ'd in sedentary Business; which would be a mighty profit to the Nation by sending those Men to Employments, where hands and Strength are more requir'd, especially at this time when we are in such want of People.

Source: Judith Drake, *An Essay in Defence of the Female Sex* (1696), section 2, pp. 9–17.

## Document 25

### Rose Hickman

*Rose Hickman, who died in 1613, left a manuscript autobiographical account of her experiences as the wife of a Protestant merchant in the mid-sixteenth century.*

Afterwards my husband (to drive away the wicked days) went to Antwerp, where he had a fair house which he rented for £40 a year, and I being with child went into Oxfordshire to a gentleman's house that was a lodge and stood far off from any church or town (the name whereof was Chilswell) and there I was delivered. And from thence I sent to Oxford to the bishops (who were then and there in prison, and did afterwards suffer martyrdom there) to be advised by them whether I might suffer my child to be baptized after the popish manner: who answered me that the sacrament of baptism, as it was used by the papists, was the least corrupted, and therefore I might. But therewithal they said that I might have been gone out of England before that time, if I had done well. And so my child was there baptized by a popish priest but because I would avoid the popish stuff as much as I could, I did not put salt into the handkerchief that was to be delivered to the priest at the baptism, but put sugar in it instead of salt.

Source: Maria Dowling and Joy Shakespeare, 'Religion and Politics in mid-Tudor England through the eyes of an English Protestant Woman: The Recollections of Rose Hickman', *Bulletin of the Institute of Historical Research* 55 (1982), p. 100.

## Document 26

### Alice Driver

*Foxe's Book of Martyrs recorded the story of Alice Driver, executed at Ipswich in 1558 alongside Alexander Gouche. This is the first of two examinations.*

**The examination of Driver's wife, before Dr Spenser the Chancellor of Norwich.**

First, she coming into the place where she should be examined, with a smiling countenance, Dr Spenser said: Why woman, dost thou laugh us to scorn?

**Driver's wife.** Whether I do, or no, I might well enough, to see what fools ye be.

**Dr Spenser.** Then the Chancellor asked her wherefore she was brought before him, and why she was laid in prison.

**Dri.** Wherefore I think I need not to tell you: for ye know it better than I.

**Spenser.** No by my troth woman, I know not why.

**Dri.** Then have ye done me much wrong (quoth she) thus to imprison me, and know no cause why: for I know no evil that I have done, I thank God, and I hope there is no man that can accuse me of any notorious fact that I have done justly:

**Spenser.** Woman, woman, what saiest thou to the blessed Sacrament of the altar? Dost thou not believe that it is very flesh and blood, after the words be spoken of consecration?

Driver's wife at those words held her peace, and made no answer. Then a great chuff headed priest that stood by, spake, and asked her why she made not the Chancellor an answer. With that, the said Driver's wife looked upon him austerely, and said: Why priest, I come not to talk with thee, but I come to talk with thy master: but if thou wilt I shall talk with thee, command thy master to hold his peace. And with that ye priest put his nose in his cap, and spake never a word more. Then the Chancellor bade her make answer to that he demanded of her.

**Dri.** Sir, said she, pardon me though I make no answer, for I cannot tell what you mean thereby; for in all my life I never heard nor read of any such Sacrament in all the Scripture.

**Spenser.** Why, what scriptures have you read, I pray you?

**Dri.** I have (I thank God) read God's book.

**Spenser.** Why, what manner of book is that you call God's book?

**Dri.** It is the old and new Testament. What call you it?

**Spenser.** That is God's book indeed, I cannot deny.

**Dri.** That same book have I read throughout, but yet never could find any such sacrament there: and for that cause I cannot make you answer to that thing I know not. Notwithstanding, for all that, I will grant you a sacrament, called the Lord's supper: and therefore seeing I have granted you a Sacrament, I pray you shew me what a sacrament is.

**Spenser.** It is a sign. And one D. Gascoine being by, confirmed the same, that it was the sign of an holy thing.

**Dri.** You have said the truth sir, said she. It is a sign indeed, I must needs grant it: and therefore seeing it is a sign, it cannot be the thing signified also. Thus far we do agree: for I have granted your own saying.

Then stood up the said Gascoine, and made an oration with many fair words, but little to purpose, both offensive and odious to the minds of the godly. In the end of which long tale, he asked her if she did not believe the omnipotency of God, and that he was almighty, and able to perform that he spake. She answered, yes, and said I do believe that God is almighty, and able to perform that he spake and promised.

**Gasc.** Very well. Then he said to his disciples: Take, eat, this is my body: Ergo, it was his body. For he was able to performed that he spake, and God useth not to lie.

**Dri.** I pray you did he ever make any such promise to his disciples, that he would make the bread his body?

**Gasc.** Those be the words. Can you deny it?

**Dri.** No, they be the very words indeed, I cannot deny it: but I pray you, was it not bread that he gave unto them?

**Gasc.** No, it was his body.

**Dri.** Then was it his body that they did eat over night?

**Gasc.** Yea, it was his body.

**Dri.** What body was it then that was crucified the next day?

**Gasc.** It was Christ's body.

**Dri.** How could that be, when his disciples had eaten him up over night? except he had two bodies, as by your argument he had: one they did eat over night, and another was crucified the next day. Such a doctor, such doctrine. Be you not ashamed to teach the people, that Christ had two bodies? In the 22. of Luke, He took bread and brake it, and gave it to his disciples, saying, Take, etc. and do this in the remembrance of me. St Paul also saith, 1. Cor 11, Do this in the remembrance of me: for as often as ye shall eat this bread, and drink this cup, ye shall shew the Lords death till he come: and therefore I marvel ye blush not before all this people, to lie so manifestly as ye do.

With that Gascoine held his peace, and made her no answer: for, as it seemed, he was ashamed of his doings. Then the Chancellor lift up his head from his cushion, and commanded the gaoler to take her away.

**Dri.** Now, said she, ye be not able to resist the truth, ye command me to prison again. Well, the Lord in the end that judge our cause, and to him I leave it. Iwisse, Iwisse, this gear will go for no payment then. So went she with the gaoler away.

Source: John Foxe, *Actes and Monuments of these Latter and Perilous Dayes* (1583), Book 12, pp. 2048–9, retrieved from *The Unabridged Acts and Monuments Online* (Digital Humanities Institute, Sheffield, 2011), www.dhi.ac.uk/foxe/ [accessed 01.02.22].

## Document 27

### John Dod and Robert Cleaver

*Puritan preachers John Dod and Robert Cleaver's 400-odd page volume of domestic advice enlarged from biblical precepts was first published in 1598 and reprinted eight times. Its length made it prohibitive to all but the social elite, but its ideas would have been widely familiar from sermons and homilies. The following extract is from the sections on the duty of husbands to wives.*

The duty of the husband is to get goods: and of the wife to gather them together, and save them. The duty of the husband is to travel abroad, to seek living: and the wife's duty is to keep the house. The duty of the husband is to get money and provision: and of the wives, not vainly to spend it. The duty of the husband is to deal with many men: and of the wives to talk with few. The duty of the husband is to be intermeddling: and of the wife, to be solitary and withdrawn. The duty of the man is, to be skilful in talk: and of wife, to boast of silence. The duty of the husband is to be a giver: and of the wife, to be a saver. The duty of the man is, to apparel himself as he may: and of the woman, as it becometh her. The duty of the husband, is to be lord of all: and of the wife, to give account of all. The duty of the husband is, to dispatch all things without door: and of the wife, to oversee and give order for all things within the house. Now, where the husband and wife performeth these duties in their house, we may call it a college of quietness: the house wherein these are neglected, we may term it a hell.

It is to be noted, and noted again, that as the provision of household dependeth only on the husband: even so the honour of all dependeth only of the woman: in such sort, that there is no honour within the house, longer than a man's wife is honourable. And therefore the Apostle calleth the woman, *The glory of the man*. But here it must be noted and remembered, that we do not entitle honourable to such, as be only beautiful, comely of face, of gentility, of comely personage, and a good housewife: but only, to her that is virtuous, honest of life, temperate, and advised in her speech.

...

Therefore the husband without any exception, is master over all the house, and hath more to do in his house with his owne domestical affaires, then the magistrate. The wife is ruler over all other things, but yet under her husband. There are certain things in the house that only do appertain to the authority of the husband, wherewith it were a reproach for the wife, without the consent of her husband, to meddle: as to receive strangers, or to marry her daughter. But there are other things, in the which the husband giveth over his right unto his wife: as to rule and govern her maidens: to see to those things that belong unto the kitchen, and to housewifery, and to their household stuff. Other mean things, as to buy and sell certain necessary things, may be ordered after the wit, wisdom, and fidelity of the woman.

*Source*: John Dod and Robert Cleaver, *A Godly Forme of Household Government* (1621), chap. 1.


# Document 28

## Homily of the State of Matrimony

*Extracts from the homily on matrimony, probably by Bishop John Jewell, which appeared in the second volume of homilies published by the Elizabethan*

*Church in 1571, to be preached in place of a sermon. The preceding section discusses the miseries of unhappy marriage.*

Learn thou therefore, if thou desirest to be void of all these miseries, if thou desirest to live peaceably and comfortably in wedlock, how to make thy earnest prayer to God, that he would govern both your hearts by his holy spirit, to restrain the devil's power, whereby your concord may remain perpetually. But to this prayer must be joined a singular diligence, whereof St Peter giveth this precept, saying, You husbands, deal with your weaker vessel, and as unto them that are heirs also of the grace of life, that your prayers be not hindered. This precept doth particularly pertain to the husband: for he ought to be the leader and author of love, in cherishing and increasing concord, which then shall take place, if he will use moderation and not tyranny, and if he yield some thing to the woman. For the woman is a weak creature, not endued with like strength and constancy of mind, therefore they be the sooner disquieted, and they be the more prone to all weak affections and dispositions of mind, more than men be, and lighter they be, and more vain in their fantasies and opinions. These things must be considered of the man, that he be not too stiff, so that he ought to wink at some things, and must gently expound all things, and to forbear. Howbeit the common sort of men doeth judge, that such moderation should not become a man: For they say that it is a token of womanish cowardness, and therefore they think that it is a man's part to fume in anger, to fight with fist and staff. Howbeit, howsoever they imagine, undoubtedly St Peter doth better judge what should be seeming to a man, and what he should most reasonably perform. For he saith, reasoning should be used, and not fighting. Yea he saith more, that the woman ought to have a certain honour attributed to her, that is to say, she must be spared and borne with, the rather for that she is the weaker vessel, of a frail heart, inconstant, and with a word soon stirred to wrath. And therefore considering these her frailties, she is to be the rather spared. By this means, thou shalt not only nourish concord: but shalt have her heart in thy power and will.

   ...

   Now as concerning the wife's duty. What shall become her? Shall she abuse the gentleness and humanity of her husband and, at her pleasure, turn all things upside down? No surely. For that is far repugnant against God's commandment, For thus doeth St Peter preach to them, Ye wives, be ye in subjection to obey your own husbands. To obey, is another thing than to control or command, which yet they may doe, to their children, and to their family: But as for their husbands, them must they obey, and cease from commanding, and perform subjection. For this surely doth nourish concord very much, when the wife is ready at hand at her husband's commandment, when she will apply her self to his will, when she endeavoureth her self to seek his contentation, and to do him pleasure, when she will eschew all things that might offend him: For thus will most truly be verified the saying of the poet, A good wife by obeying her husband, shall bear the rule, so that he shall have a delight and a gladness, the sooner at all times to return home to her. But on the contrary part, when the wives be stubborn, froward, and malapert, their husbands are compelled thereby to abhor and flee from their own houses, even as they should have battle with their enemies. Howbeit, it can scantly be, but that some offences shall sometime chance betwixt them: For no man doth live without fault, specially for that the woman is the more frail party. Therefore let them beware that they stand not in their faults and wilfulness: but rather let them acknowledge their follies, and say, My husband, so it is, that by my anger I was compelled to do this or that forgive it me, and hereafter I will take better heed. Thus ought the woman more readily to do, the more they be ready to offend. And they shall not do this only to avoid strife and debate: but rather in the respect of the commandment of God, as St Paul expresseth it in this form of words, Let women be subject to their husbands as to the Lord: for the husband is the head of the woman, as Christ is the head of the Church. Here you understand, that God hath commanded that ye should acknowledge the authority of the husband, and refer to him the honour of obedience. And Saint Peter saith in that place before rehearsed, that holy matrons did in former time deck themselves, not with gold and silver, but in putting their whole hope in God, and in obeying their husbands, as Sara obeyed Abraham, calling him lord, whose daughters ye be (saith he) if ye follow her example. This sentence is very meet for women to print in their remembrance. Truth it is, that they must specially feel the grief and pains of their Matrimony, in that they relinquish the liberty of their own rule, in the pain of their travailing, in the bringing up of their children. In which offices they be in great perils, and be grieved with great afflictions, which they might be without if they lived out of Matrimony.

...

This let the wife have ever in mind, the rather admonished thereto by the apparel of her head, whereby is signified, that she is under covert or obedience of her husband as that apparel is of nature so appointed, to declare her subjection: so biddeth Saint Paul that all other of her raiment should express both shamefastness and sobriety. For if it be not lawful for the woman to have her head bare, but to bear thereon the sign of her power, wheresoever she goeth: more is it required that she declare the thing that is meant thereby. And therefore these ancient women of the old world called their husbands lords, and shewed them reverence in obeying them ...

...

But yet I mean not that a man should beat his wife, God forbid that, for that is the greatest shame that can be, not so much to her that is beaten, as to him that doth the deed, but if by such fortune thou chancest upon such an husband, take it not too heavily, but suppose thou, that thereby is laid up no small reward hereafter, and in this life time no small commendation to thee, if thou canst be quiet. But yet to you that be men, thus I speak, Let there be none so grievous fault to compel you to beat your wives. But what say I your wives, no, it is not to be born with, that an honest man should lay hands on his maid servant to beat her. Wherefore if it be a great shame for a man to beat his bondservant, much more rebuke it is, to lay violent hands upon his freewoman. And this thing may be well understood by the laws which the Painims hath made, which doth discharge her any longer to dwell with such an husband, as unworthy to have any further company with her that doth smite her.

Source: *The Second Tome of Homilies of Such Matters as Were Promised, and Intituled in the Former part of Homilees. Set out by the Authoritie of the Queenes Maiestie: and to Be Read in euery Parishe Church Agreeably* (1571), pp. 476–89.

## Document 29

### Dorothy Leigh

*Dorothy Leigh's advice to her sons was first published in 1616, after her death, and reprinted numerous times. These sections address her motherhood as cause for writing and publishing; her celebration of the Virgin Mary, as part of advice on how to name children; and her advice to her sons on how to treat their wives.*

### Chap. 2 'The First Cause of Writing, is a Motherly Affection'

But lest you should marvel, my children, why I do not, according to the usual custom of women, exhort you by word and admonitions, rather then by writing, a thing so unusual among us, and especially in such a time, when there bee so many godly books in the world, that they mould in some men's studies, while their Masters are marred, because they will not meditate upon them; as many men's garments motheate in their chests, while their Christian brethren quake with cold in the street for want of covering; know therefore, that it was the motherly affection that I bare unto you all, which made me now (as it often hath done heretofore) forget my self in regard of you: neither care I what you or any shall think of me, if among many words I may write but one sentence, which may make you labour for the spiritual food of the soul, which must be gathered every day out of the word, as the children of Israel gathered Manna in the wilderness.

### Chap. 3 'The Best Labour Is for the Food of the Soul'

...

My dear Children, have I not cause to fear? the holy Ghost saith by the Prophet, *Can a Mother forget the child of her womb?* As if he should say, Is it possible, that she, which hath carried her child within her, so near her heart, and brought it forth into this world with so much bitter pain, so many groans and cries, can forget it? nay rather, will shee not labour now till Christ be formed in it? will shee not bless it every time it sucks on her breasts, when she feeleth the blood come from her heart to nourish it? Will she not instruct it in the youth, and admonish it in the age, and pray for it continually? Will she not be afraid, that the child which shee endured such pain for, should endure endless pain in hell? Could Saint *Paul* say unto the *Galatians,* that were but strangers to him concerning the flesh, only he had spent some time amongst them to bring them to the profession of the truth, from which he feared they would fall: and could he, I say, write unto them, *My little children, of whom I doe travail again in birth, until Christ be formed in you?* And can any man blame a mother (who indeed brought forth her childe with much pain) though she labour again till Christ bee formed in them? Could S. *Paul* wish himself separated from God for his brethren's sake and will not a mother venture to offend the world for her children's sake? Therefore let no man blame a mother, though she something exceed in writing to her children, since every man knows, that the love of a mother to her children, is hardly contained within the bounds of reason.

*Chap. 9 'The Seventh Cause Is, that they Should Give their Children Good Names'*

... It may be, that some of you will marvel, since I set down names for the imitation of their virtues, that bore them; why I placed not *Mary* in the first place, a woman virtuous above all other women. My reason was this, because I presumed, that there was no woman so senseless, as not to look what a blessing God hath sent to us women through that gracious Virgin, by whom it pleased God to take away the shame, which Eve our Grandmother had brought us to: For before, men might say, The woman beguiled me, and I did eat the poisoned fruit of disobedience, and I die. But now man may say, if he say truly, The woman brought me a Saviour, and I feed of him by faith and live. Here is this great and woeful shame taken from women by God, working in a woman: man can claim no part in it: the shame is taken from us, and from our posterity for ever: *The seed of the woman hath taken down the Serpent's head*; and now whosoever can take hold of the seed of the woman by faith, shall surely live for ever. And therefore all generations shall say, that she was blessed, who brought vs a Saviour, the fruit of obedience, that whosoever feedeth of, shall live forever: and except they feed of the seed of the woman, they have no life. Will not therefore all women seek out this great grace of God, that by *Mary* hath taken away the shame, which before was due unto us ever since the fall of man?

Source: Dorothy Leigh, *The Mother's Blessing; or The Godly Counsel of a Gentle-woman, not Long since Deceased, Left Behinde her for her Children* (1621).

# Document 30

*Maria Thynne*

*Aged sixteen, Maria Touchet and Thomas Thynne married secretly in 1594, apparently supported by her mother, and a long family legal battle ensued. This letter from around 1604 may be suggesting pregnancy ('piamater').*

Mine own sweet Thomken, I have no longer ago than the very last night written such a large volume in praise of thy kindness to me, thy dogs, thy hawks,
the hare and the foxes, and also in commendation of thy great care of thy
businesses in the country, that I think I need not amplify any more on that text,
for I have crowned thee for an admirable good husband with poetical laurel,
and admired the inexpressible singularity of thy love in the cogitations of *piamater*, I can say no more but that in way of gratuity, the dogs shall without
interruption expel their excremental corruption in the best room (which is thy
bed) whensoever full feeding makes their bellies ache, and for my own part
since you have in all your letters given me authority to care enough, I will
promise to be inferior to none of my Deverill neighbours in playing the good
housewife, though they strive till they stink. Now if for my better encouragement and in requital thou will at my earnest entreaty but for this time spare
Digory, I shall be so much bound, that nothing but a strong purgation can
loose me. For if you will believe me in sober sadness, my cousin Stantor hath
upon speech with me, made it appear that he hath digested many uncivil and
unbecoming words from three of your servants. He doth not desire you to
remit Digory's fault, but to dispense with his appearance for his sake this
time, because it concerns him in his profit, and when you come into the
country my cousin will come and thoroughly satisfy all matters in controversy
between you. I will not entreat too earnestly because I known thou art choleric with me ever in these cases, but though thou doth many times call me
fool for yielding to the enticing of fair words, yet if you mark it, I have never
yet craved anything of such great importance as hath ever been prejudicial to
your reputation or profit. If so (as it is too true it is so) name me any man that
hath a wife of that rare temper. No, in good faith this age will not help you to
an equal, I mean for a wife. Alas I sit at home and let thy dogs eat part with
me, and wear clothes that have worn out their prenticeship a year and half
sithence; when my sisters will be in London at their pleasure, I am talking of
foxes and ruder beasts at home. Well, do but make haste home and make
much of thy Mall when thou dost come home. I will not be melancholy, but
with good courage spend my life and waste my spirits in any course to lease
thee, except fighting, and in this business satisfy my request as you think I
deserve, and do not be angry with me for importuning you, but ask all the
husbands in London, or ask the question in the Lower House, what requests
they grant their wives, and then good husband think upon your fool at home
as there is cause.

    Thine,

    Maria Thynne.

    I will say nothing of any business, for I have this last night written you a
whole sheet of paper and given you knowledge, according to your appoint-
ments, of all your affairs. If your leisure will not serve, good sweet, cause Exall
to write in his own name but this and this is my mistress' pleasure and it shall
serve the turn, for I know your trouble in matters of more weight there is great,

and I like not his writing in your name for it is as though thou were angry. God in heaven send thee well and speedily home.

Source: *Two Elizabethan Women: Correspondence of Joan and Maria Thynne 1575–1611*, ed. Alison D. Wall (Devizes: Wiltshire Record Society, 1983), pp. 32–3.

## Document 31

### Elizabeth Freke

*Elizabeth Freke (1642–1714), a Norfolk gentlewoman, left two successive versions of 'Some few remembrances of my misfortunes that have attended me in my unhappy life since I were married'. She started writing in 1702; the earlier entries are probably made with reference to previous notes. Married in 1672 by choice and for love to a cousin, Percy Freke, she recorded a married life beset with struggles to keep her land and money intact from her husband's debts and borrowing. This extract records her father's attempt to help her, and three years later, her exile in Bilney, the Norfolk house that she held in trust for her son.*

**July 7** [1682] So soon as I came to my dear father, he made me promise him that I would not leave him whilst I lived, which I readily and gladly did. And then he bid me take no care for I should want for nothing his life, who made his words good with the greatest kindness to me and my son. A great alteration it was to what I found in Ireland from a husband.

**August 15** And on my looking a little melancholy on some past reflections, he fancied it was my want of money; and my dear father, without saying a word to me, went up into his closet and brought me down presently in two bags two hundred pounds, which £200 he charged me to keep private from my husband's knowledge and buy needles and pins with it. This was very kind in my father; and which the very next post I informed Mr Freke of, who presently found a use for it. But I, that had not two and twenty shillings from my husband in the last two and twenty months I were in Ireland with my son, kept it for my own use. Which with more my father had given me and the interest, all which made up eight hundred pounds, [Mr Freke] took from me the year after my son married and so left me at Bilney a beggar again.

...

**December 24** [1685] Mr Freke came over by Dublin from Ireland, I having hardly heard of him or from him in three quarters of a year. As he came unlooked for by me, so he was very angry with me for being on this side of the country, though in all his times of his being from me he never took care for a penny for my subsistence or his sons. For which God forgive him. My husband's errand for England was to join with him in the sale of West Bilney to Sir Standish Hartstonge for the like in Ireland. But I being left the only trustee for my self and my son, God gave me the courage to keep what I had rather than part with it and be kept by the charity of my friends or trust to his or any one's kindness. So in a great anger Mr Freke left me alone again and went for Ireland, where he stayed from me almost two years.

Source: *The Remembrances of Elizabeth Freke, 1671–1714*, ed. Raymond
A. Anselment, Camden Society, fifth series, volume 18 (Cambridge:
Cambridge University Press, 2001), pp. 49, 55.

## Document 32

### Anne and James Young

*Anne Young, née Lingham, sued her husband James for separation at the London consistory court in 1608, on the grounds of his cruelty to her. The following documents represent one of her witnesses' statements, and his response to her claims. (Italic sections are translated from Latin.)*

Margaret Bonefant, *wife of James Bonefant, woolman, of St Olave Southwark, whose wife she has been for about 12 years; she has been married to him 12 years and is about 32; she has known Anne Young for 9 or 10 years and James Young for 3 months.*

... *To the 2nd and 3rd articles she deposes and says* that in the month of February last past upon a Sunday in the afternoon ... this deponent went to the articulate Anne Young alias Lingham to her own house in St Bride's parish in London to visit her and to see how she did and coming to her she found the said Anne Young alias Lingham so beaten and bruised and swollen about her head face and body that she was not able to speak nor go nor stir any of her limbs to help her self and her jaws were displaced or otherwise so hurt with beating that she was not able to stir them and the gristle of her nose was so bruised that until by the help of a surgeon it was raised and the flesh suppled she could not well fetch or take any breath at the nose, but seemed as though she were more like to die of that beating than to recover and live. And soon after that this jurate came and saw the said Anne in this miserable case the said James Young her husband came in, to whom this Jurate said she was sorry to see his wife in this miserable case. Whereunto he answered that he did think her estate had been better when he married her than he did then find it as he said and then she this deponent asking him if he had so used her, he said that that which was done to her he had done, and so she this deponent then said unto him that was not the way to know or understand of her estate but if he would know that it must be his kind usage of her and not that severity for that was a way to make an end of them both. 'Aye', quoth he the same Young, 'I am told I shall be hanged if she die within a year and a day but if I be there is but one out of the way'. And this speech of his acknowledging his so beating of his said wife he the same Young did avouch once or twice after within as then a week after walking with this deponent in the street homeward towards her this deponent's house in St Olave's parish from his the same Young's house. And she saith there was present and saw her the same Anne Young alias Lingham in that pitiful sort as aforesaid, Mrs Anne Cotes one Mr Grace and divers others ...

*To the 5th she says* that both at the time afore by her deposed of upon the Sunday and twice after the same week when she this deponent came to see her the same Ann Young alias Lingham she hath been in sad want as that she this deponent did see Mrs Cotes and others that came to her give her money and send for drink wood and coals and for meat and likewise for ointments for her and for diverse things that was fit for her comfort she having no money her self but being in great want and need ...

*To the 6th article she says* that for the reasons by her deposed of she saith that she verily believeth and that not without cause the said Anne dareth not nor may not live safely with her said husband in one house for fear of death or at least such cruel usage as she is not able to ...

*To the 13th* ... she saith she never heard any body ever say better of him than that he was and is such a severe cruel man to his wife.

*To the 14th she says* that at such time as the articulate James Young and his said wife lay in her this deponent's house ... he hath acknowledged and confessed both to her this deponent and in her hearing that he was worth four hundred pounds ...

Ann Cotes, *wife of Edward Cotes of St Dunstan in the West, poulterer, where she has lived for 18 years and more, born in Buckinghamshire, aged 37... she has known Anne Young for 26 years and James Young since Michaelmas last.*

*To the first article of the said libel she says and deposes* that she this deponent doth know that the articulate James Young and Alice Young alias Lingham are commonly accounted lawful man and wife together and so have been ever since about Michaelmas last or a little before ...

*To the 2 and 3 articles ... she says and deposes* that in the month of February and about the beginning of February last as she now remembreth the time otherwise she remembreth not, one Sara a maidservant of the articulate James Young and his wife came to her this deponent being a neighbour, by her and told her that her master and mistress were fallen out and that they being alone in the house, 'I fear' quoth she 'that he will kill her or do her some great mischief, he hath thrust me out at doors', whereupon she this deponent going thither did then find her the same Ann Young alias Lingham articulate in a most pitiful case so beaten about the face and head that her cheeks and part of her face by her nose were swollen above her nose and is black as a black sloe the gristle of her nose (as it seemed) broken, and she said that she had sent for a surgeon that had lifted it up for before he had done so she told her this deponent that she could not speak and it seemed to be true the face and nose was so exceedingly battered and bruised insomuch as she was so weak and in such a pitiful case as she this deponent and all the women that were there did verily think she would have died as she this deponent thinketh she will ever hardly recover it for thereby and ever since she hath used to have such strange fits of shaking and quaking as that she is for the time when the fit cometh blind and senseless very strange to see. And this deponent so seeing her at that time she talked with James Young her husband then there present who confessed unto her this deponent that he had so broken her and that she was in that sort by his breaking of her but seemed not to be sorry or care for it ...

*To the 5th article she says* that both the time afore by her deposed of and sundry times since she this deponent seeing her the articulate Anne Young to be in need of sustenance she saith that she this deponent hath given her money to send her such necessaries as she wanted both meat drink firing and such like ...

*To the 6th article she says* that she does not know ... saving she saith that ... when she found Anne Young cruelly beaten as aforesaid she the same Anne Young said in presence of her said husband that he would have run at her with a rapier or sword that was there and she this deponent telling him of it and reproving him for that his cruel using of his wife he did not deny it or gainsay it but seemed to ratify it to be true ...

*Personal Answers of James Young*

6 June 1608

*To the 2nd and 3rd articles he responds* that Ann Young this respondent's wife articulate having given him this respondent many vile and bad speeches, he this respondent hath sundry times in the time articulate chidden her and given her many angry words again. And he saith that the week before Shrovetide last she ... having taken up a thing of wood like unto a bowl to strike him this respondent, he this respondent saith that he did strike her the same Ann with his fist in so much as her face was black and blue. Whereupon she the same Ann forsook his this respondent's bed, and that night the next following lay by her self and the next morning he this respondent going up into her chamber and seeing her purse lying there took out two rings or three that was in it and when she arose and found that he this respondent had taken away her rings she became so sullen that she counterfeited her self sick and went to bed and kept her bed a week after whereby she caused him this respondent to spend 40 s. in keeping of her in that her counterfeit sickness.

*To the 4th he responds* that the same day that he this respondent did so strike his said wife presently after one Mistress Cotes one of his said wife's acquaintance being there told him this respondent that if his wife did otherwise than well he this respondent should be hanged whereupon he this respondent said unto her that if she would not be quiet she might and it were well she were gone out at doors, but she went away none the sooner ...

*To the 8th and 9th he responds* that such hath, been and was the wickedness of the articulate Ann his this respondent's said wife towards him this respondent as that she hath divers times when he this respondent hath gone out of doors she hath fallen down of her knees and prayed to God that he this respondent might never come in at the doors again whereby this respondent was in a desperate mind about the time articulate for which he is now heartily sorry and desireth almighty God to forgive him as that in the morning when he arose out of his bed (he lying alone as he had done long before and after his said wife refusing his company) he did stab himself with a knife which he carrieth to bed with him in the breast in two places.

*To the 14th he responds* that he this respondent is a tailor and getteth thereby 2s. 6d. a week and not above 3s. and is not worth forty shillings his debts paid but he saith that if his said wife would be quiet and live quietly with him in the face of God as he this respondent desireth to do he doubteth not but he should get much more and be better able to keep and maintain both himself and her than now he is to keep himself his mind is so unquiet by reason of this trouble.

Source: London Metropolitan Archives DL/C 218, pp. 50–2, 88.

## Document 33

### Joan Vokins

*Joan Vokins, a Quaker, travelled to America and the Caribbean in the late seventeenth century; these two passages, including her letter home to her brother Oliver, were published after her death, a common practice to remember Quaker lives.*

And then I being clear, and a passage presented for Barbados, as soon as I was ready I went aboard, and was there sooner than could have been expected: And when I arrived, I met with many Friends at Bridgetown, and there took an account of the Monthly Meetings, and went to them and other Meetings as brief as I could; and most Days I had two or three Meetings of a Day, both among the Blacks, and also among the White People: And the Power of the Lord Jesus was mightily manifested, so that my Soul was often melted therewith, even in the Meetings of the Negro's or Blacks, as well as among Friends.
...

### To Oliver Sansom and his Wife

Dear Brother and Sister,

Whom I dearly love in the Lord Jesus, (our Life) who makes hard things easy, bitter things sweet, and bears up in the greatest Trials, do I salute you, with my Mary, my Sister Margery, and the rest of them, earnestly desiring your Prosperity every way, as for my own Soul. And by this you may know, that tho' sore Exercises and Travels attend on every hand; yet I am alive to magnify that Power that hath preserved in Dangers great, and Difficulties many, and is able to Preserve unto the end, and therefore I desire that we may trust in it, and obey it, to the honour of it; for it hath been manifest in my weak Body, to the admiration of many of the upright in Heart, and they are very Loving to me where ever I come: And my tender Father hath strengthened me to do his Service in Long-Island, and New-York, and in Road-Island, and Boston, and New-

Jersey, and those parts of America, and I was in hope to have come home when I was clear of New England; but the Lord hath laid it upon me to go to Barbados, and in his Strength I am going on in a Vessel that one George Fletcher is Owner and Master of, who professes Truth. Do you not think that a Line from you would be very precious to me? I neither heard from, nor saw one of my Native Land since I left it; but I cannot blame you, not knowing whither to direct it. Remember my dear Love to all dear Friends of our Men's and Women's Meetings, earnestly desiring their Faithfulness therein, and in all things else that pertains to the life of Truth, that we may bear our Testimonies in Uprightness unto the end, that in the end God may be glorified, and our Souls comforted, for ever and evermore. Dear Anne Lawrence's Children be in my Mind as well as my own: I hope you will look after them in my Absence, that we may have comfort of their Growth in the Truth, if ever we are present again; and if they grow in the Truth, and Knowledge, and Love of God, then will the Desire of your tender Sister be answered. And so in that which satisfies our Breathings, I remain,

Your Tender Sister, J. V.

The 1st of the Eighth Month, 1680

Source: Joan Vokins, *God's Mighty Power Magnified as Manifested and Revealed in his Faithful Handmaid Joan Vokins* (London, 1691), pp. 43, 54.

## Document 34

### *The Law's Resolutions of Women's Rights*

*An anonymous text of 1632,* The Lawes Resolutions of Womens Rights, *thought to be by barrister Sir John Dodderidge, outlined the property, marital and other legal positions of women, distinguishing carefully between the single and the married. These sections deal with property.*

### Section VIII 'That which the Husband Hath is his Own'

But the prerogative of the husband is best discerned in his dominion over all external things in which the wife by combination divesteth herself of propriety in some sort, and casteth it upon her governor, for here practice everywhere agrees with the theoricke of law, and forcing necessity submits women to the affection thereof, whatsoever the husband had before coverture either in goods or lands, it is absolutely his own, the wife hath therein no seisin at all. If anything when he is married be given him, he taketh it by himself distinctly to himself.

If a man have right and title to enter into lands, and the tenant enfeoff the baron and feme, the wife taketh nothing. Dyer fol. 10. The very goods which a man giveth to his wife, are still his own, her chain, her bracelets, her apparel are all the goodman's goods.

If a woman taketh more apparel when her husband dieth than is necessarily for her degree, it makes her executrix *de son tort demesne, 33. H6.* A wife how gallant soever she be, glistereth but in the riches of her husband, as the moon hath no light, but it is the sun's. Yea and her Phoebe borroweth sometime her own proper light from Phoebus.

### Section IX 'That which the Wife Hath is the Husband's'

For thus it is, if before marriage the woman were possessed of horses, meat, sheep, corn, wool, money, plate and jewels, all manner of moveable substance is presently by conjunction the husband's, to sell, keep or bequeath if he die; and though he bequeath them not, yet are they the husband's executor's and not the wife's which brought them to her husband.

Source: *The Lawes Resolutions of Womens Rights* (1632), pp. 129–30.

# Document 35

### Edward Barlow

*Edward Barlow was born at Prestwich, near Manchester, in 1642. At fourteen he was apprenticed to a whitester (whitening yarn and fustians) but he left his service, dissatisfied with the conditions; these extracts from a long journal, written from memory in later life, tell of his perceptions of the household he worked in, and then of his decision to leave home to go to sea.*

Moreover I perceived my master to be of a hasty nature, and my dame none of the best conditions as I judged by her looks; also they had a great many children, some of them grown to marriage estate, which made me think that ere long I should have more masters and dames than one. Likewise I considered their manner of keeping two tables of victuals. Though we all ate together, yet at the upper end of the table, where my master and dame and the children did sit, there was a great difference of victuals, namely a pudding with suet and plums; but at the lower end of the table one without both, though there might be a little strong butter to eat with it, melted and poured upon it: and at the upper end a piece of fat beef, but at the lower end a piece of sirloin next to the horns: there was always something or other which we had not. We also had meat broth two or three times heated, which would never have vexed me had I eaten and drunk of the same as they did, though I had not sat at table with them.

My fellow servant would also be telling me how many broils and combustions he had had with my master and dame about their beating of him. Some of the neighbours told him in my hearing that he deserved his master's daughter for a wife for his good services to him, which made me think he might take her in God's name, for I did not care for buying a wife at so dear a rate as to serve apprenticeship for her, which might not prove worth a man's labour at cost of marrying her.

... [He leaves the position and returns home, shortly to leave again for London.]

So coming down the stairs, my mother and one of my sisters being in the house and not knowing my intent, marvelled to see me put on my clothes that day. Passing by them, not staring at all, I bid them farewell and came out of the house. They sat still awhile to see whither I would go, and by and by when I was gotten almost out of call, my mother came out, and seeing that I did intend to go, called to me in the manner you see here drawn, beckoning her hand to come again, and willing me not to go I could not tell whither, and if I would go, to stay till my father came home and see what he would say to it. Yet with all her persuasions she could not entreat me to stay; but away I came to my father. He, seeing me coming, asked me whither I intended to go. I told him to London to see if I could get me a place to live in; and I desired him to lend me the six shillings upon my part of the fowling piece, for I did hope to trouble him no more, and [told him] that he might take it upon my partner or else give him six shillings more and take the fowling piece to himself. So my father considering of it lent it me and said if I would I might go in God's name: and bid me have a care of myself that I did not come into a worse place than that which he had provided for me at the whitesters, where I would not stay; and so prayed God to bless me. And I came away with tears in my eyes and (in my pocket) that sum of six shillings and one or two shillings more that I had of my own, which I had gotten before I went to my master's of some of our neighbours by working by the day for twopence and threepence a day.

Considering with myself I decided I had as good to go seek my fortune abroad as live at home, always in want and working hard for very small gains. Likewise I had never any great mind to country work, as ploughing and sowing and making of hay and reaping, nor also of winter work, as hedging and ditching and thrashing and dunging amongst cattle, and such-like drudgery. And I thought I had as good go see what I could, knowing that it could not be much worse wheresoever I came, and that any rate I should be out of the ill-will of some of our neighbours. Some of them would not venture a day's journey from out of the smoke of their chimneys or the taste of their mother's milk; not even upon the condition that they might eat and drink of as good cheer as the best nobleman in the land, but they would rather stay at home and eat a brown crust and drink a little whey.

Source: Edward Barlow, *Barlow's Journal of His Life at Sea in King's Ships, East and West Indiamen and Other Merchantmen from 1659 to 1703*, 2 vols, ed. Alfred Basil Lubbock (Hurst and Blackett, 1934), vol. 1, pp. 20–21.

Document 36

## Searchers of the Dead

*In the plague outbreaks of the late sixteenth and early seventeenth centuries, the City of London issued orders for coping with infection. These clauses prescribe the provision of women as searchers of bodies.*

That the churchwardens and constable in every precinct, provide, and have in readiness, one, or more sober discreet women, as the case shall require to be providers and deliverers of necessaries for the infected houses, and to attend the persons sick and infected, at the charge of such householders of such houses, if they be able: and if not, then at the charge of the parish. And that such women once entering into charge of such provision and attendance, shall carry red wands, go by the channel side, and forbear assemblies, as is aforesaid.

...

That in or for every parish there shall be appointed two sober ancient women, to be sworn to be viewers of the bodies of such as shall die in time of infection, and two other to be viewers of such as shall be sick, and suspected of infection, which women shall immediately upon such their views, by virtue of their oath, make true report to the Constable of that precinct, where such person shall die, or be infected, to the intent that true notice may be given both to the Alderman or his deputy, and to the Clerk of the Parish, and from him to the Clerk of the Parish Clerks, that true certificate may be made as hath been used. And that every of the said women, Constable, or Clerk, failing in the premises, shall suffer imprisonment as is aforesaid. And every woman so sworn, and for any corruption, or other respect falsely reporting, shall stand upon the pillory, and bear corporal pain by the judgement of the Lord Mayor and Court of Aldermen. They at their going abroad to bear red wands, go near the channel, and shun assemblies, as before.

That every woman, or other appointed to any service for the infected, and refusing, or failing to do that service, shall not have any pension out of the hospital or parish.

Source: *Orders to Be Used in the Time of the Infection of the Plague within the Citie and Liberties of London* (1625).

## Document 37

### The Infanticide Act

*Passed in 1624, this implied an epidemic of infanticide among single mothers.*

*An Act to Prevent the Destroying and Murdering of Bastard Children*

Whereas many lewd women that have been delivered of bastard children, to avoid their shame, and to escape punishment, do secretly bury or conceal the death of their children, and after, if the child be found dead, the said women do allege, that the said child was born dead; whereas it falleth out sometimes (although hardly it is to be proved) that the said child or children were murdered by the said women, their lewd mothers, or by their assent or procurement:

For the preventing therefore of this great mischief, be it enacted by the authority of this present Parliament, That if any woman after one month next ensuing the end of this session of Parliament be delivered of any issue of her body, male or female, which being born alive, should by the laws of this realm be a bastard, and that she endeavour privately, either by drowning or by secret burying thereof, or any other way, either by herself or the procuring of others, so to conceal the death thereof, as that it may not come to light, whether it were born alive or not, but be concealed: In every such case the said mother so offending shall suffer death as in case of murder, except such mother can make proof by one witness at the least, that the child (whose death was by her so intended to be concealed) was born dead.

Source: 21 Jac.I c. 27, Statutes of the Realm.

## Document 38

*William Brandling*

*Two men were prosecuted by the church in Durham in 1563 for fighting in the churchyard.*

*The Examination of William Brandling, of Newcastle, Mariner, Aged 36 years, to Articles against Him*

He saith that, upon Saturday at night next before the day articulate, this examinate and the said George was at drink in one Mother Blithman's in the said town; at what time in the end they two cast words; and the said George offered to fight with this examinate; and thereupon the place was appointed the morrow next after in the morning, where this deponent was, but not the said George. And afterward, this examinate meeting the said George Keidland in the said church yard, said that he did not well to brag and crack and appoint a place to fight and would not come. To whom the said George answered and said that he would be with him, this examinate, by and by; and therewith the said George ran in unto his father Robert Keidland's house and brought forth a great staff, and therewith smote at this examinate and felled him, being upon the church stile and one, this, out of the church yard and th'other on the church stile, the said George being then in the said church yard, saying that the blood did more issue forth of this examinate.

*Janet Doods, of Newcastle, Single Woman, Aged 30 Years*

This examinate did see all those there in the place articulate, betwixt ten and eleven of the clock, upon one Sunday three weeks past and more. She did hear the said Robert Keidland speak unseeming words in the church yard to the said William Brandling, saying 'Scots mongrel, thou dare not smite my son'. George Keidland smote and made bloody the said William Brandling with a staff, when old Keidland held the said William. She did see the said Robert also bled, but she cannot tell by what means.

Source: Depositions and Other Ecclesiastical Proceedings from the Courts<br>of Durham, ed. James Raine, Surtees Society 21 (J. B. Nichols and<br>Son, 1845), pp. 74–6.

## Document 39

### Elizabeth Bromley and Edith Griffyn

*A deposition from a defamation case sued between two women at the London church court in 1566. Sections in italics are translated from the Latin.*

*Repeated in front of the bishop's official on the 18 November 1566 in the presence of me William Blakwell notary*

Marion Johnson, *wife of Francis Johnson, of the parish of St Giles in the Fields, where she has lived for 6 years and before that at Grindon Underwood, Bucks for 2 years, born at Simpson in the same county, aged about 40, and says she testifies freely. Examined first as to her knowledge of the parties she has known Elizabeth Bromley for 6 years and Edith Griffyn alias Mayne well since the time of Quadragesima last.*

*To the first she says that the contents of this one are true.*

*To the second by virtue of her oath she says and deposes* that upon a certain day happening about midsummer last past before this her examination ... and in the afternoon of the same day the articulate Elizabeth Bromley came home to this deponent's house being situated by the Strand within the parish of St Giles in the Field where she this deponent and the articulate Elizabeth Bromley sitting at her door and talking together Edith Griffyn articulate, being next neighbour unto this deponent and espying the said goodwife Bromley, came to her and said unto her 'Thou burdenest me that I should steal a saw and a pair of shoes out of Mr Darbie's shop. But' quoth the said Edith 'thou art a whore and an arrant whore and if thou didst as I do thou wouldst not be so fat nor maintained by other women's husbands and the best in the town will say that thou art an arrant whore.' Then being present and hearing the premises this deponent Margaret Boothe and Elizabeth Reynoldes with divers of the neighbours thereabouts whose names this deponent remembreth not...

Source: London Metropolitan Archives, DL/C/210 fos 6<sup>v</sup>–7<sup>v</sup>.

# Document 40

## *Nehemiah Wallington*

*Nehemiah Wallington (1598–1658) was a London woodturner. In the numerous notebooks he left recording his reflections on life, his conduct and sense of self is driven by his Puritan beliefs. In this extract from a notebook entitled 'The Growth of a Christian' he expresses his helplessness in the face of the wrong 'done unto religion', but also to his standing in the community, by a dishonest apprentice.*

On the second of May [1641] I went to the sacrament and found some comfort. But this month I had as sad a thing befallen me as ever I had in my life for it pierced me to my soul. For my man William had sold some trenchers and told the customer they were maple when they were aspen which was a lie and I did sharply reprove him for it. And when the customer was gone my neighbour's man called the customer and told her that we had cozened her. And a day after the gentlewoman came to me and told me my man had cozened her and had sold her aspen trenchers for maple and that his sin was mine and that I ought to make good what wrong my man doth. And they say you are a religious man but you will lie and cozen so that you bring a slander on Religion and I partly know you for an honest man and that you have lived under a faithful minister a long time which makes your sin so much the greater. Then I answered all this I know and for the wrong he hath done to you it shall be no loss to you for I will return all your money to you again but as for the wrong he hath done unto Religion I can no way help it.

Source: *The Notebooks of Nehemiah Wallington, 1618–1654: A Selection,*
ed. David Booy (Aldershot: Ashgate, 2007), p. 151.

# Document 41

## *Isabel Montera de Gamboa*

*This document from London's church court records the dilemma of a Portuguese woman in London. Isabel Montera de Gamboa had been captured and enslaved from the Azores by North African pirates, and then ransomed in Algiers by James Frissell, the English Consul. They then married, but discovered that her previous husband was still alive; court proceedings were necessary to resolve the situation. Her testimony was translated from Portuguese by the contemporary interpreter.*

**The personal answers of Isabella Montera de Gamboa, alias Ferreira, alias Frissell, to the articles presented on behalf of James Frissell, interpreted by William Breame**

To the first article she responds that about eleven years since and within the time articulate this respondent and the articulate Francis Ferreira articulate being free from all former contracts of matrimony as she believeth did contract pure and lawful matrimony as she believeth and procured the banns therefore to be asked in the church of our Lady the Assumption being the principal church in the Island of St Mary's in Portugal, and afterwards the said marriage was solemnized publicly between them this respondent and the said Francis Ferreira on a Sunday in the afternoon about three of the clock at the time of evening prayer according to the rites and ceremonies of the said church of the said Island of St Mary's in Portugal, and the said marriage was so solemnized at the high altar in the said church in the presence of divers people and namely one John Swaver and others as she believeth, and further believeth that this respondent and the said Francis Ferreira did consummate the same marriage by having the carnal use and knowledge of each other's bodies and this respondent had two children begotten of her body by the said Francis Ferreira as she believeth ...

To the second article she responds and believes that after the solemnization of the said marriage this respondent and the said Francis Ferreira lived together in the island articulate as man and wife for the space of three years and not above as she believes, and for man and wife were then and there commonly accounted reputed and taken as she believes ...

To the third article she responds and believes that about the time articulate the said Francis Ferreira went to sea as master's mate of a ship to Brazil and was absent a year as she believes and then returned to the island of St Mary's again where he found this respondent and then the said Francis when he had stayed there some seven or eight months went to sea again in another voyage to Brazil again as she believes and the ship went in being laden with sugar and cast away on the coast of Brazil as she believes when she was coming homewards to St Mary's as she believes and that thereupon news came to the said island that the said Francis was drowned in the sea as she believes ...

To the fourth article she responds and believes that before the return of the said Francis Ferreira in the second voyage the Turks invaded the said island of St Mary's and took this respondent amongst others captive and carried her to the Algiers and in the year articulate as she believes and set this respondent amongst others to sale for a slave as she believes ...

To the sixth article she responds and believes that it was told this respondent for a certain truth before she was taken captive and lived in St Mary's and afterwards when she was in the Algiers that her said husband the said Frances Ferreira was dead ...

To the seventh article she responds and believes that this respondent came from the Algiers with the said James Frissell to this realm of England and after their arrival here it was related to the articulate James and this respondent by letters from beyond the seas that the said Francis Ferreira her this respondent's husband was dead. And thereupon this respondent and the said James Frissell about the time articulate did contract matrimony and were married in the parish church of St Margaret within Westminster according to the rites and ceremonies of the Church of England by virtue of a licence obtained in that behalf as she believes and did after consummate the same by carnal copulation and hath had ~~three~~ five children begotten of her body by the said James whereof she had two at a birth as she believes ...

To the eighth article she responds and believes that the said James Frissell and this respondent were certified both by letter and by relation of the articulate Anthony Ferreira, the brother of this respondent's said husband Francis Ferreira which Anthony is now in England, that the said Francis Ferreira was living at the time of the solemnization of the marriage between this respondent and the articulate James Frissell which report she doth now believe to be true and saith she hath heard he was in March last at the Terceiras articulate ...

[signed with X]

Source: London Metropolitan Archives, DL/C 228, f. 328 (9 Oct 1622)

## Document 42

### Elizabeth Poole

*Elizabeth Poole joined the Particular Baptist sect in her teens and in the late 1640s, in her mid- twenties, prophesied to the Council of the New Model Army. This published pamphlet records her second meeting with them, advising them against regicide and drawing on the familiar language of patriarchalism.*

Dear Sirs,

Having already found so free admission into your presences it hath given me the greater encouragement (though more peculiarly, the truth persuading me thereunto) to present you with my thoughts in these following lines. I am in divine pleasure made sensible of the might of the affairs which lye upon you; and the Spirit of sympathy abiding in me, constraineth me to groan with you in your pains. You may remember I told you the Kingly power is undoubtedly fallen into your hands, which power is to punish evil-doers, and to praise them that do well: Now therefore my humble advice to you is, that you stand as in the awful presence of the most high Father, acting your parts before God and man, you stand in the place of interpreters, for many hard sayings present themselves to you, and will doe, look for it: wherefore see,

That you give unto men the things that are theirs, and upon God the things that are his, it is true indeed, as unto men (I know I appeal by the gift of God upon me) the King is your Father and husband, which you were and are to obey in the Lord, and no other way, for when he forgot his Subordination to divine Faithhood and headship, thinking he had begotten you a generation to his own pleasure, and taking you a wife for his own lusts, thereby is the yoke taken from your necks.

Wherefore put your swords into his hands for your defence, and fear not to act the part of Abigail, seeing Nabal hath refused it (by Appropriating his goods to himself) in relieving David and his men in their distress; it was to her praise, it shall be to yours, fear it not: Only consider, that as she lifted not her hand against her husband to take his life, no more do ye against yours...

You never heard that a wife might put away her husband, as he is the head of her body, but for the Lord's sake suffereth his terror to her flesh, though she be free in the spirit to the Lord; and he being uncapable to act as her husband, she acteth in his stead; and having the spirit of Union abiding in her, she considereth him in his temptations, as tempted with him: And if he will usurp over her, she appealeth to the Fatherhood for her offence, which is the spirit of justice, and is in you; For I know no power in England to whom it is committed, save yourselves (and the present Parliament) which are to act in the Church of Christ, as she by the gift of faith upon her, shall be your guide for the cure of her body, that you might therefore commit an unsound member to Satan (though the head) as it is flesh; that the spirit might be saved in the day of the Lord (I believe). And accordingly you may hold the hands of your husband, that he pierce not your bowels with a knife or sword to take your life.

Source: Elizabeth Poole, *A Vision: Wherein Is Manifested the Disease and Cure of the Kingdom* (1649).

## Document 43

### *Sir Thomas Smith*

*Smith was a scholar, MP, and trusted adviser of Elizabeth I. His account of her commonwealth, which became a standard work, emphasised the participatory aspects of governance that protected against tyranny, whilst excluding ordinary women from any part in office-holding.*

### *Chapter 16 'The Division of the Parts and Persons of the Commonwealth'*

To make all things yet clear before, as we shall go, there ariseth another division of the parts of the commonwealth. For it is not enough to say that it consisteth of a multitude of houses and families which make streets and villages, and the multitude of the streets and villages make towns, and the multitude of towns the realm, and that freeman be considered only in this behalf, as subjects and citizens of the commonwealth, and not bondmen who can bear no rule nor jurisdiction over freemen, as they who be taken but as instruments and the goods and possessions of others. In which consideration also we do reject women, as those whom nature hath made to keep home and to nourish their family and children, and not to meddle with matters abroad, nor to bear office in a city or common wealth no more than children and infants: except it be in such cases as the authority is annexed to the blood and progeny, as the crown, a duchy, or an earldom for there the blood is respected, not the age nor the sex. Whereby an absolute Queen, an absolute Duchess or Countess, those I call absolute, which have the name, not by being married to a king, duke, or earl, but by being the true, right and next successors in the dignity, and upon whom by right of the blood that title is descended: These I say have the same authority although they be women or children in that kingdom, duchy or earldom, as they should have had if they had been men of full age. For the right and honour of the blood, and the quietness and surety of the realm, is more to be considered, than either the tender age as yet impotent to rule, or the sex not accustomed (otherwise) to intermeddle with public affairs, being by common intendment understood, that such personages never do lack the counsel of such grave and discreet men as be able to supply all other defects.

> Source: Thomas Smith, *De Republica Anglorum: The Manner of Government or Policy of the Realm of England* (1583), pp. 18–19.

## Document 44

### Lucy Hutchinson

*Lucy Hutchinson's memoir of the life of her husband John, one of the parliamentary leaders in the Civil War, recorded their opinions of Charles I.*

But above all these the king had another instigator of his own violent purpose, more powerful than all the rest, and that was the queen, who, grown out of her childhood, began to turn her mind from those vain extravagancies she lived in at first, to that which did less become her, and was more fatal to the kingdom; which is never in any place happy where the hands which were made only for distaffs affect the management of sceptres. – If any one object the fresh example of Queen Elizabeth, let them remember that the felicity of her reign was the effect of her submission to her masculine and wise counsellors; but wherever male princes are so effeminate as to suffer women of foreign birth and different religions to intermeddle with the affairs of state, it is always found to produce sad desolations; and it hath been observed that a French queen never brought any happiness to England. Some kind of fatality, too, the English imagined to be in her name of Marie, which, it is said, the king rather chose to have her called by than her other, Henrietta, because the land should find a blessing in that name, which had been more unfortunate; but it was not in his power, though a great prince, to control destiny. This lady being by her priests affected with the meritoriousness of advancing her own religion, whose principle it is to subvert all other, applied that way her great wit and parts, and the power her haughty spirit kept over her husband, who was enslaved in his affection only to her, though she had no more passion for him than what served to promote her designs.

> Source: Lucy Hutchinson, *Memoirs of the Life of Colonel Hutchinson, Governor of Nottingham* (London: John C. Nimmo, 1885), vol. I, pp. 125–6.

## Document 45

### *Alice Baine and Dorothy Dawson*

*These extracts are from a Star Chamber suit about a protest against the enclosure of fifty acres of ground on Grewelthorpe Moor in Yorkshire by the Puritan gentleman Sir Stephen Proctor. While Proctor elsewhere alleged the women's behaviour was masterminded by their husbands, the bill of complaint claimed that Dawson was known as 'Captain Dorothy' for her rude and riotous behaviour. Many of those involved were middle-aged married women. The witnesses are answering interrogatories posed by Proctor, the plaintiff.*

**Alice Baine, wife of Roger Baine of Grewelthorpe in the county of Yorkshire, about the age of 44 years, sworn and examined, deposeth as followeth.**

To the first she saith that Dorothy Dawson, Jane Walton, Luce Walker, Dorothy Lie, Ellen Walker, Isabel Baines, Francis Dunne, Jennett Adamson, Jane Burniston and this examinant with others whom she cannot remember about the time mentioned in this interrogatory did assemble themselves on Grewelthorpe moor, and did cast down a piece of a fence begun by the complainants to be enclosed near the coal pits, and the quantity so thrown down at that time exceeded not to her thinking a yard and a half in measure, and there was a man on the said ground, whose name she knoweth not, neither to whom he did belong, neither was he working at that time to her remembrance.

To the second she saith that she knoweth not who did move or procure the said women first to throw down the said ditch or to go to the said moor at that time when the ditch was so cast down, but saith it was a matter of general grievance to them, and did not know, one more willing than another, but the persons aforenamed did all go together to pull down some little part of the said ditch, that they might thereby have their commons as before; And saith for her own part she did not make her husband privy to the intention, neither was she willed or moved by her said husband to do the same, neither knoweth any other thing mentioned in this Interrogatory.

**Dorothy Dawson wife of Richard Dawson of Grewelthorpe aforesaid, about the age of 44, sworn and examined, deposeth as followeth ...**

To the third she saith that about the time mentioned in this interrogatory this examinant and Alice Baines went at one time to the said moor where the fifty acres mentioned in this interrogatory was in hand to be enclosed to have made a hap for their cattle into the said ground and there put down a sod or two with their hands not carrying any weapons nor drawing any knives and the workman being there present did interrupt this examinant and the other at that time to pull down any more of the said ditch, and so they went quietly home at that time. And shortly after within a day or two, the said Elizabeth Branston a very poor woman being great with child came to this deponent, and said that she had but one cow and if she might not go on the moor she were beggared, for she had no money to set her with at grass, and requested this deponent to go with her to pull down a gap to let her cow go into the said enclosure. At whose entreaty she this examinant went and there finding nobody to resist they two with their hands did pull down a gap, which when they had done and returning home again six of the complainants' servants or workfolks came forth of a house near to the enclosure, and running after them overtook them and drew them back again to the place which they had thrown in, and offering to throw the said Elizabeth Branston into a ditch being full of water, and three quarters in depth this examinant offered to help the said woman and being holden by one John Branley this examinant got hold of the said Elizabeth Branston with one hand, and of him that would have thrown her in the ditch with the other hand, and pulled out a piece of his coat that so held the said woman, and the same fellow did rive the said Elizabeth Branston's coats which if it had not riven he had thrown her into the ditch, and she verily thinketh that the said Elizabeth Branston got her death by that struggling, for she then told this examinant that they had given her that which she could never cast, and shortly after the said Elizabeth died. But this examinant or any other to her knowledge did not strike with knives the said Branley nor pulled him by the hair of the head but only touched him when he held her and she further saith that this examinant's husband was privy to her going when they went but two together for the pulling of the said ditches in such manner as is beforehand only for passing of their cattle.

Source: *Proctor v Dawson et al.* (1608), The National Archives, STAC8/227/3.

## Document 46

### Brilliana Harley

*Lady Brilliana Harley, the third wife of Lord Robert Harley, wrote to him in 1643 when he was in London and she was in Herefordshire with one of their sons, Ned, defending their castle, Brampton Bryan, against royalist forces. She died a month later of a cold.*

24 Sept 1643

My Dear Sir

I hope before this you have heard by Proser that the Lord has been gracious to us, and has sent our enemies away from before Brampton: for which great goodness of our God to us his poor despised servants, I hope you and the rest who prayed for us will now help us to praise our God for his great mercy to us never to be forgotten.

On Saturday last the 23 of this month I received your letter by Fischer in which you advise me to come away from Brampton.

Dear Sir, hitherto God has made me (though an unworthy one) an instrument to keep possession of your house that it has not fallen into the hands of spoilers, and to keep together a handful of those such as feared the Lord together so that his word has yet had an abiding in these parts, which if the Lord remove Herefordshire is miserable. In this work I have not thought my life dear, neither shall I.

Sir could Ned Harley come down I should think myself to have much comfort, and I think he would do his country service and himself good in helping to keep what I hope shall be his, and in maintaining the Gospel in this place, Oh let me beg of you to take poor Herefordshire into consideration and commiseration, if the faithful ministry be removed and carried up to London so as they are, what shall become of the country, I think it had been a thousand times better if Mr Yarts had stayed in the Country for upon his going away there is a popish minister crowded in here I have still disavowed his being there and as far as I can I suffer him not to have the benefit of the place neither dare he abide there, if please you to send Mr Banyte a commission from the parliament to take possession of it he would and I believe the people would be glad of him.

To my sorrow I hear Mr Gower has accepted of another place at London. If so let me desire you to place another in Brampton by the mystery of the Parliament or else there will some wicked one get in.

Sir my Lord of Essex is gone from Gloucester so that I cannot expect a convoy from him and by this enclosure you may see what I may expect from Gloucester.

If my son could come down I should hope we might comfortably keep what we have left, if that can not be then I pray you think how some commission may be granted that some strength may be raised.

Sir the man you write of to entrust your house with if I should have followed his counsel it had been gone. Therefore I do not think he would keep it. Mr Banyte is of an opinion that if please God I go away, it will not be long kept not that I do any great matter but I have something more authority and should have more care than any other.

My dear Sir I pray you consider all things and do not look upon me as if I were afraid but what you would have me do in that which may be best for you, and that I shall most gladly do, all my pleasures are in you and then I must be most pleased when you are pleased. And therefore dear Sir think what you would have me do and let me know it and I shall be best pleased to do that.

This bearer can relate all passages to you and I hope you will hasten him out of town.

I might begin a new letter in letting you know how good God has been to me in all things he has exceedingly blessed the provisions of my house so that it has held out beyond expectation.

I thank God the children are all well and all in my house

Dear Sir when you write to Colonel Massy give him thanks for the kindness he shows to me

I beseech the Lord to preserve you and to give you a happy meeting with her that begs your love and prays for [you]

Your most affectionate wife

Brilliana Harley

Sir I sent to you a great while ago for a gown I pray you will you send me one I desire it may be silk cheap made up plain I believe my [torn]s measure will serve me and my cousin Davis's men may bring it down

Sept 24 1643

Brampton Castle

Source: British Library Ms Add 70110.

## Document 47

### Abiezer Coppe

*Abiezer Coppe (1619–1672),* **Ranter** *and prophet, published this exchange between himself and a female follower in a collection of epistles in 1649. The first is from 'Mrs. T. P.', and goes on to describe a vision of beasts and fish; the second is Coppe's reply.*

Dear Brother,

My true love in the spirit of one-ness, presented to your self – with all that call on the name of the Lord; both yours and ours. It hath pleased The Father of late, so sweetly to manifest his love to my soul, that I cannot but return it to you, who are the image of my Father.

I should rejoice, if the Father pleased also, to see you, and to have some spiritual communion with you, that I might impart those soul-ravishing consolations, which have flown from the bosoms of the Father, to our mutual comfort. What though we are weaker vessels, women etc. yet strength shall abound, and we shall mount up with wings as eagles; we shall walk, and not be weary, run and not faint, when the man-child Jesus is brought forth in us. Oh what a tedious, faint way have we been led about to find out our rest, and yet when all was done, we were twice more the sons of slavery then – But blessed be our God, who hath brought us by a way that we know not, and we are quickly arrived at our rest.

...

Dear Sister, in the best fellowship, mine entire love, etc. presupposed –

I have received your letter, and the Father's voice in it, but it came not into our coast till the 12 of November, which was the Fathers time, since which time, I have scarce been one whole day at home, but abroad, at my Meat and Drink – so (that if I durst, yet) I could not so much as plunder an opportunity, – but now it is freely given me to write. –

I know you are a vessel of the Lord's house, filled with heavenly liquor, and I see your love, – The Father's love, in the sweet returns of your (I mean) his sweets to me. I love the vessel well, but the wine better, even that wine, which we are drinking new, in the Kingdom.

And it is the voice of my Beloved, that saith, drink oh friends! yea, drink abundantly oh Beloved!

Dear friend, why dost in thy letter say, [what though we are weaker vessels, women? etc] I know that Male and Female are all one in Christ, and they are all one to me. I had as lief hear a daughter, as a son prophesy. And I know, that women, who stay at home, divide the spoil – whilst our younger brethren, who are (as we were) abroad, and not yet arrived at our Father's house, or are at home, are spending their substance in riotous living, and would fain fill their bellies with husks; the outside of the grain.

Source: Abiezer Coppe, *Some Sweet Sips, of Some Spirituall Wine* (1649),<br>Epistles IV and V, pp. 39–40, 45–6.

## Document 48

*Petition of the Gentlewomen and Tradesmen's Wives*

*This petition, presented to Parliament in early 1642 by a group of women led by Mrs Anne Stagg, a brewer's wife, and printed shortly afterwards, spoke in the voice of working women to urge Parliament to press the King to purge the kingdom of Catholicism. Earlier on, it details the alleged atrocities in Ireland, including rape and murder; this section concludes the seven-page document with a discussion of the rights of petitioning.*

*To the Honourable Knights, Citizens and Burgesses, of the House of Commons assembled in Parliament. The most humble Petition of the Gentlewomen, Tradesmen's wives, and many others of the Female Sex, all Inhabitants of the City of London, and the Suburbs thereof.*

With lowest submission shewing,

That we also with all thankful humility acknowledging the unwearied pains, care and great charge, besides hazard of health and life, which you the noble worthies of this honourable and renowned assembly have undergone, for the safety both of church and commonwealth, for a long time already past; for which not only we your humble petitioners, and all well affected in this kingdom, but also all other good Christians are bound now and at all times to acknowledge; yet not withstanding that many worthy deeds have been done by you, great danger and fear do still attend us, and will, as long as popish lords and superstitious bishops are suffered to have their voice in the House of Peers, and that accursed and abominable idol of the mass suffered in the kingdom, and that arch-enemy of our prosperity and Reformation lieth in the Tower, yet not receiving his deserved punishment.

All these under correction, gives us great cause to suspect, that God is angry with us, and to be the chief causes why your pious endeavours for a further Reformation proceedeth not with that success as you desire, and is most earnestly prayed for of all that wish well to true religion, and the flourishing estate both of King and kingdom; the insolencies of the papists and their abettors, raiseth a just fear and suspicion of sowing sedition, and breaking out into bloody persecution in this kingdom, as they have done in Ireland, the thoughts of which sad and barbarous events, maketh our tender hearts to melt within us, forcing us humbly to petition to this honourable Assembly, to make safe provision for your selves and us, before it be too late.

And whereas we, whose hearts have joined cheerfully with all those Petitions which have been exhibited unto you in the behalf of the purity of religion, and the liberty of our husbands' persons and estates, recounting our selves to have an interest in the common privileges with them, do with the same confidence assure our selves to find the same gracious acceptance with you, for easing of those grievances, which in regard of our frail condition, do more nearly concern us, and do deeply terrify our souls: our domestical dangers with which this kingdom is so much distracted, especially growing on us from those treacherous and wicked attempts already are such, as we find ourselves to have as deepen a share as any other.

We cannot but tremble at the very thoughts of the horrid and hideous facts which modesty forbids us now to name, occasioned by the bloody wars in Germany, his Majesty's late northern army, how often did it affright our hearts, whilst their violence began to break out so furiously upon the persons of those, whose husbands or parents were not able to rescue: we wish we had no cause to speak of those insolencies, and savage usage and unheard of rapes, exercised upon our sex in Ireland, and have we not just cause to fear they will prove the forerunners of our ruin, except Almighty God by the wisdom and care of this Parliament be pleased to succour us, our husbands and children, which are as dear and tender unto us, as the lives and blood of our hearts, to see them murthered and mangled and cut in pieces before our eyes, to see our children dashed against the stones, and the mothers' milk mingled with the infants' blood, running down the streets; to see our houses on flaming fire over our heads: oh how dreadful would this be! We thought it misery enough (though nothing to that we have just cause to fear) but few years since for some of our sex, by unjust divisions from their bosom comforts, to be rendered in a manner widows, and the children fatherless, husbands were imprisoned from the society of their wives, even against the laws of God and Nature; and little infants suffered in their fathers' banishments: thousands of our dearest friends have been compelled to fly from episcopal persecutions into desert places amongst wild beasts, there finding more favour than in their native soil, and in the midst of all their sorrows, such hath the pity of the prelates been, that our cries could never enter into their ears or hearts, nor yet through multitudes of obstructions could never have access or come nigh to those royal mercies of our most gracious Sovereign, which we confidently hope, would have relieved us: but after all these pressures ended, we humbly signify, that our present fears are, that unless the blood-thirsty faction of the papists and prelates be hindered in their designs, our selves here in England as well as they in Ireland, shall be exposed to that misery which is more intolerable than that which is already past, as namely to the rage not of men alone, but of devils incarnate, (as we may so say) besides the thraldom of our souls and consciences in matters concerning God, which of all things are most dear unto us.

Now the remembrance of all these fearful accidents aforementioned, do strongly move us from the example of the woman of Tekoa to fall submissively at the feet of his Majesty, our dread Sovereign, and cry Help O King, help o ye the noble worthies now sitting in Parliament: And we humbly beseech you, that you will be a means to his Majesty and the House of Peers, that they will be pleased to take our heart breaking grievances into timely consideration, and to add strength and encouragement to your noble endeavours, and further that you would move his Majesty with our humble requests, that he would be graciously pleased according to the example of the good King Asa, to purge both the court and kingdom of that great idolatrous service of the Mass, which is tolerated in the Queen's court, this sin (as we conceive) is able to draw down a greater curse upon the whole kingdom, then all your noble and pious endeavours can prevent, which was the cause that the good and pious King Asa would not suffer idolatry in his own mother, whose example if it shall please his Majesty's gracious goodness to follow, in putting down popery and idolatry both in great and small, in court and in the kingdom throughout, to subdue the papists and their abetters, and by taking away the power of the prelates, whose government by long and woeful experience we have found to be against the liberty of our conscience and the freedom of the Gospel, and the sincere profession and practice thereof, then shall our fears be removed, and we may expect that God will power down his blessings in abundance both upon his Majesty, and upon this Honourable Assembly, and upon the whole land.

For which your new petitioners shall pray affectionately.

*The Reasons follow.*

It may be thought strange, and unbeseeming our sex to shew our selves by way of Petition to this Honourable Assembly: but the matter being rightly considered, of the right and interest we have in the common and public cause of the Church, it will, as we conceive (under correction) be found a duty commanded and required.

First, because Christ hath purchased us at as dear a rate as he hath done Men, and therefore requireth the like obedience for the same mercy as of men.

Secondly, because in the free enjoying of Christ in his own Laws, and a flourishing estate of the Church and Common-wealth, consisteth the happiness of Women as well as Men.

Thirdly, because Women are sharers in the common Calamities that accompany both Church and Common-Wealth, when oppression is exercised over the Church or Kingdom wherein they live; and an unlimited power have been given to Prelates to exercise authority over the Consciences of Women, as well as Men; witness Newgate, Smithfield, and other places of persecution, wherein Women as well as Men have felt the smart of their fury.

Neither are we left without example in Scripture, for when the state of the Church, in the time of King Ahasuerus was by the bloody enemies thereof sought to be utterly destroyed, we find that Esther the Queen and her maids fasted and prayed, and that Esther petitioned to the King in the behalf of the Church: and though she enterprised this duty with the hazard of her own life, being contrary to the Law to appear before the King before she were sent for, yet her love to the Church carried her through all difficulties, to the performance of that duty.

On which grounds we are emboldened to present our humble Petition unto this Honourable Assembly, not weighing the reproaches which may and are by many cast upon us, who (not well weighing the premises) scoff and deride our good intent. We do it not out of any self-conceit, or pride of heart, as seeking to equal ourselves with men, either in authority or wisdom: But according to our places to discharge that duty we owe to God and the cause of the Church, as far as lieth in us, following herein the example of the men, which have gone in this duty before us.

A relation of the manner how it was delivered, with their answer, sent by Mr. *Pym*.

*This Petition, with their Reasons, was delivered the 4th of Feb. 1641. by Mrs Anne Stagg, a Gentlewoman and Brewers Wife, and many others with her of like rank and quality, which when they had delivered it, after some time spent in reading of it, the Honourable Assembly sent them an Answer by Mr Pym, which was performed in this manner.*

*Mr Pym came to the Commons door, and called for the Women, and spake unto them in these words*: Good Women, your Petition and the reasons have been read in the House; and is very thankfully accepted of, and is come in a seasonable time. You shall (God willing) receive from us all the satisfaction which we can possibly give to your just and lawful desires. We intreat you to repair to your houses, and turn your Petition which you have delivered here, into Prayers at home for us, for we have been, are, and shall be (to our utmost power) ready to relive you, your husbands, and children, and to perform the trust committed unto us, towards God, our King and Country, as becometh faithful Christians and loyal subjects.

Source: *A True Copie of the Petition of the Gentlewomen and Tradesmens-Wives, in and about the City of London Delivered to the Honourable, the Knights, Citizens, and Burgesses of the House of Commons in Parliament, the 4th of February, 1641 (1642), pp. 5–6.*

# Glossary

**£, s., d.**  Pounds, shillings, pence. 12 d. = 1 shilling; 20 shillings = £1.

**Benefit of clergy**  A legal fiction by which, after 1575, a felon capable of reading a verse from the Bible could be excused hanging. It was extended to women in 1624.

**Bridewell**  Prison in London, governed by summary justice, which received arrestees from constables and other offices and punished them with work and whipping.

**Chancery**  High court of equity, offering an alternative to common law based on principles of justice rather than precedent, largely concerned with civil matters such as land.

**Charivari**  Customary parade, also called skimmington ride, often involving 'rough music' with pots and pans.

**Church courts**  Courts enforcing canon law via litigation or disciplinary prosecutions, overseen by bishop.

**Churchwardens**  Elected unpaid lay officials of each parish, responsible for law and order in the church, poor relief and church maintenance.

**Constable**  Unpaid parish official, working at the orders of justices of the peace.

**Court of Requests**  Minor equity court, popular in the late sixteenth century due to its cheap fees and fast process.

**Coverture**  The common law doctrine whereby a married woman's legal identity was subsumed under that of her husband.

**Feme sole**  In law French, the legal status of a single woman.

**Mosaic law**  Laws attributed to Moses, set out in the first five books of the Old Testament.

**Mother**  Sometimes used to mean womb.

**National Covenant**  Scottish agreement against Charles I's church reforms.

**Protestation Oath**  Oath of allegiance to Charles I and the Church of England, crafted by Parliament in 1641 in an attempt to avoid the Civil War.

**Puritan**  Protestants advocating greater purity of doctrine and worship.

**Quakers**  The Religious Society of Friends, founded late 1640s, with the belief in direct relationships with God.

**Ranters** Religious dissenting group active 1649–60, who saw God in every creature and rejected obedience and hierarchy.

**Rump Parliament** The remaining parliament after the purge, in 1648, of MPs opposed to trying Charles I for treason.

**Societies for the Reformation of Manners** Began in London in 1691, mobilising associations of gentlemen, tradesmen, constables and informers to prosecute vice.

**Solemn League and Covenant** Agreement between the Scottish Covenanters and the English Parliamentarians in 1643 to defend religious reform.

**Terms** Menstrual periods.

**Tories** Opponents of Exclusion; monarchists; supporters of the Church of England.

**Whigs** Originally those supporting the exclusion of the Duke of York, eventually James II, from the throne in 1679–81.

# Guide to Further Reading

Many primary sources for researching early modern women and gender are widely available online and in print. Printed collections of sources on women's history include Patricia Crawford and Laura Gowing (eds), *Women's Worlds in Seventeenth-Century England* (London: Routledge, 2000), and Helen Ostovich and Elizabeth Sauer (eds), *Reading Early Modern Women: An Anthology of Texts in Manuscript and Print, 1550–1700* (London: Taylor & Francis, 2004). Several editions of legal records, rich in women's depositions, have been reprinted in paperback, and are often also available online; for example, James Raine (ed.), *Depositions and Other Ecclesiastical Proceedings from the Courts of Durham*, Surtees Society 21 (Durham, 1845), and James Raine (ed.), *Depositions from the Castle of York, relating to offences committed in the Northern Counties in the seventeenth century*, Surtees Society 40 (Durham, 1861). An extraordinary body of medical and psychological notes, with many queries from women, is digitally available via the Casebooks Project (https://casebooks.lib.cam.ac.uk). Printed books by (and about) women are almost all available on Early Modern Books (Proquest) and ballads about courtship, marriage, crime, or war at the English Broadside Ballad Archive (http://ebba.english.ucsb.edu). The Old Bailey Online (www.oldbaileyonline.org) is a fully searchable resource of the court records for felonies that were printed in London from the 1680s onwards. London Lives (www.londonlives.org) also includes some Bridewell and London sessions records, and a recent project digitizing English Petitions is held at British History Online (www.british-history.ac.uk).

Of the several general books on early modern women, Sara Mendelson and Patricia Crawford's collaborative *Women in Early Modern England 1550–1720* (Oxford: Oxford University Press, 2000) still stands out, and should be read alongside the newer chapter on gender, body and sexuality by Alexandra Shepard in Keith Wrightson (ed.), *A Social History of England, 1500–1750* (Cambridge: Cambridge University Press, 2017). On masculinity, Alexandra Shepard, 'From Anxious Patriarchs to Refined Gentlemen? Manhood in Britain, circa 1500–1700', *Journal of British Studies* 44 (2005) provides a stimulating outline, along with Tim Reinke Williams, 'Manhood and Masculinity in Early Modern England', *History Compass* 12/9 (September 2014), and Shepard's book *Meanings of Manhood in Early Modern England* (Oxford: Oxford University Press, 2003).

On patriarchy and power, see Susan D. Amussen, 'The Contradictions of Patriarchy in Early Modern England', *Gender & History* 30/2 (2018). The hierarchy of sex, as understood in contemporary ideas, is laid out in Margaret Sommerville, *Sex and Subjection: Attitudes to Women in Early-Modern Society* (London: Hodder Arnold, 1995). Gender debates are examined in Cristina Malcomson and Mihoko Suzuki, *Debating Gender in Early Modern England* (Basingstoke: Palgrave Macmillan, 2002), and Hannah Dawson, 'Fighting for My Mind: Feminist Logic at the Edge of Enlightenment', *Proceedings of the Aristotelian Society* 118/3 (2018), puts Anger and Drake in a philosophical and radical context. Sarah Hutton and Lynette Hunter's pathbreaking collection *Women, Science and Medicine 1500–1700* (Stroud: Sutton, 1997) is an excellent introduction to the women in early science, and Hutton's essay in Amanda Capern (ed.), *The Routledge History of Women in Early Modern Europe* (London: Routledge, 2019) explains developments in the European context; this recent collection also has several other useful contributions.

Understandings of sex and reproduction, and the broader context of the gendered body, are examined in Mary Fissell, *Vernacular Bodies: The Politics of Reproduction in Early Modern England* (Oxford: Oxford University Press, 2006), Laura Gowing, *Common Bodies: Women, Touch and Power in Seventeenth-Century England* (New Haven, CT: Yale University Press, 2003), and essays in Sarah Toulalan and Kate Fisher (eds), *The Routledge History of Sex and the Body, 1500 to the Present* (Abingdon: Routledge, 2013). More focused studies of gendered bodies include Jennifer Jordan, '"That Ere with Age, His Strength is Utterly Decay'd": Understanding the Male Body in Early Modern England', in Kate Fisher and Sarah Toulalan (eds), *Bodies, Sex and Desire from the Renaissance to the Present* (Basingstoke: Palgrave, 2011), Sara Read, *Menstruation and the Female Body in Early Modern England* (Basingstoke: Palgrave Macmillan, 2013), and Lynn Botelho and Pat Thane (eds), *Women and Ageing in British Society Since 1500* (Harlow: Longman, 2001). Women's manners are explored in Sara Mendelson, 'The Civility of Women', in Peter Burke et al. (eds), *Civil Histories: Essays presented to Sir Keith Thomas* (Oxford: Oxford University Press, 2000), and Philip Carter analyses the forms of manly politeness in the later period in *Men and the Emergence of Polite Society: Britain 1660–1800* (Harlow: Longman, 2001).

On race and gender, see Kim Hall's foundational *Things of Darkness: Economies of Race and Gender in Early Modern England* (Ithaca, NY: Cornell University Press, 1995) and the introduction and documents in Ania Loomba and Jonathan Burton, *Race in Early Modern England: A Documentary Companion* (London: Routledge, 2007). Imtiaz Habib's *Black Lives in the English Archives, 1500–1677: Imprints of the Invisible* (Aldershot: Ashgate, 2008) presents a powerful argument about the archival evidence of England's Black population; London evidence can be found in the excellent online dataset 'Switching the Lens' at the London Metropolitan Archives online catalogue. Miranda Kaufmann's *Black Tudors: The Untold Story* (London: OneWorld, 2017) has several valuable studies of women, as do Onyeka Nubia, *England's*

*Other Countrymen: Black Tudor Society* (London: Zed Books, 2019) and Simon Newman, *Freedom-Seekers: Escaping from Slavery in Restoration London* (London: University of London Press, 2022).

The study of clothes offers a rich, gender-attentive analysis, including Susan Vincent, *Dressing the Elite: Clothes in Early Modern England* (London: Berg, 2003), David Kuchta, 'The Semiotics of Masculinity in Renaissance England', in James Turner (ed.), *Sexuality and Gender in Early Modern Europe* (Cambridge: Cambridge University Press, 1993), Sarah Bendall, 'To Write a Distick upon It: Busks and the Language of Courtship and Sexual Desire in Sixteenth- and Seventeenth-Century England', *Gender & History* 26/2 (2014), and Sarah Bendall, *Shaping Femininity: Foundation Garments, the Body and Women in Early Modern England* (London: Bloomsbury, 2021).

For an introduction to sexuality in the period, see Katherine Crawford, *European Sexualities, 1400–1800* (Cambridge: Cambridge University Press, 2007). James G. Turner, *Libertines and Radicals in Early Modern London* (Cambridge: Cambridge University Press, 2002) and Sarah Toulalan, *Imagining Sex: Pornography and Bodies in Seventeenth-Century England* survey erotic cultures; Martin Ingram, *Carnal Knowledge: Regulating Sex in England, 1470–1600* (Cambridge: Cambridge University Press, 2017) and Faramerz Dabhoiwala, 'Lust and Liberty', *Past & Present* 207 (2010) describe the very different regimes of sexual regulation at opposite ends of the period; prostitution is examined in Paul Griffiths, 'The Structure of Prostitution in Elizabethan London', *Continuity and Change* 8/1 (1993), and its criminalization via Bridewell in his *Lost Londons: Change, Crime, and Control in the Capital City, 1550–1660* (Cambridge: Cambridge University Press, 2008). Narratives of rape and consent are elegantly unpacked in Miranda Chaytor, 'Husband(ry): Narratives of Rape in the Seventeenth Century', *Gender & History* 7/3 (1995) and Garthine Walker, 'Rereading Rape and Sexual Violence in Early Modern England', *Gender & History* 10/1 (1998), while Walker's subsequent articles on rape, particularly 'Everyman or a Monster? The Rapist in Early Modern England, c.1600–1750', *History Workshop Journal* 76 (2013), explore its meanings for sexuality, masculinity and patriarchy.

On male homosexuality, the work of Alan Bray remains central, beginning with *Homosexuality in Renaissance England* (New York: Columbia University Press, 1982), while the wider world of love and friendship in relation to masculinity and queer theory is explored in Katherine O'Donnell and Michael O'Rourke (eds), *Love, Sex, Intimacy and Friendship between Men, 1550–1800* (Basingstoke: Palgrave, 2003). Randolph Trumbach's argument about the changing configurations of sexuality in the late seventeenth century is summed up in his 'Sex, Gender and Sexual Identity in Modern Culture: Male Sodomy and Female Prostitution in Enlightenment England', *Journal of the History of Sexuality* 2/2 (1991). Almost all the work on lesbianism focuses on representation, with much valuable discussion in Valerie Traub, *The Renaissance of Lesbianism in Early Modern England* (Cambridge: Cambridge University Press, 2002); see also Sarah Toulalan, 'Extraordinary Satisfactions: Lesbian Visibility in Seventeenth-

Century Pornography in England', *Gender & History* 15/1 (2003), and for a more social-historical approach, Judith M. Bennett, '"Lesbian-Like" and the Social History of Lesbianisms'. *Journal of the History of Sexuality* 9/1–2 (2000). Two recent collections offer a trans* approach to the pre-modern: Greta LaFleur, Masha Raskolnikov and Anna Klosowska (eds), *Trans Historical: Gender Plurality before the Modern* (Ithaca, NY: Cornell University Press, 2021), and Simone Chess, Colby Gordon and Will Fisher, 'Introduction: Early Modern Trans Studies', *Journal for Early Modern Cultural Studies* 19/4 (2019). Thomas/ine Hall's case is examined in Kathleen Brown, '"Changed … into the Fashion of Man": The Politics of Sexual Difference in a Seventeenth-Century Anglo-American Settlement', *Journal of the History of Sexuality* 6/2 (1995), and Amy Pulter's in Patricia Crawford and Sara H. Mendelson, 'Sexual Identities in Early Modern England: The Marriage of Two Women in 1680', *Gender & History* 7/3 (1995).

On childbirth and its rituals, see David Cressy, 'Purification, Thanksgiving and the Churching of Women in Post-Reformation England', *Past & Present* 141 (1993), Linda A. Pollock, 'Childbearing and Female Bonding in Early Modern England', *Social History* 22 (1997), and Mary E. Fissell, 'The Politics of Reproduction in the English Reformation', *Representations* 87/1 (2004). Philippa Carter, 'Childbirth, "Madness", and Bodies in History', *History Workshop Journal* 91 (2021) discusses 'frenzy', and Alexandra Shepard, 'The Pleasures and Pains of Breastfeeding in England c.1600–1800' in M. J. Braddick, Joanna Innes and Paul Slack (eds), *Suffering and Happiness in England 1550–1850: Narratives and Representations* (Oxford: Oxford University Press, 2017) examines breastfeeding as care work. Samuel Thomas, 'Early Modern Midwifery: Splitting the Profession, Connecting the History', *Journal of Social History* 43/1 (2009) is a good introduction to the history of midwifery, while Adrian Wilson, *The Making of Man-Midwifery: Childbirth in England, 1660–1770* (London: Routledge, 1995) outlines the shift at the end of the period.

On print culture, reading and writing literacy are re-examined in Eleanor Hubbard, 'Reading, Writing, and Initialing: Female Literacy in Early Modern London', *Journal of British Studies* 54/3 (2015). Pamela Allen Brown, *Better a Shrew Than a Sheep: Women, Drama, and the Culture of Jest in Early Modern England* (Ithaca, NY: Cornell University Press, 2002) and Tim Reinke-Williams, 'Misogyny, Jest-Books and Male Youth Culture in Seventeenth-Century England', *Gender & History* 21/2 (2009) examine gender in popular culture.

On the Reformation, Christine Peters, *Patterns of Piety: Women, Gender and Religion in Late Medieval and Reformation England* (Cambridge: Cambridge University Press, 2003) offers extensive evidence and a sense of the wider field; other specific aspects are explored in Megan Hickerson, 'Gospelling Sisters "goinge Up and Downe": John Foxe and Disorderly Women', *Sixteenth Century Journal* 35/4 (2005), Mary E. Fissell, 'The Politics of Reproduction in the English Reformation'. *Representations* 87/1 (2004), and Frances Dolan, *Whores of Babylon: Catholicism, Gender, and Seventeenth-Century Print Culture* (Ithaca, NY: Cornell University Press, 1999).

Households and families have a large but not very current bibliography. One useful collection is Helen Berry and Elizabeth Foyster (eds), *The Family in Early Modern England* (Cambridge: Cambridge University Press, 2007), while Will Coster's seminar study *Family and Kinship in England, 1450–1800* (London, Routledge: 2016) updates the field. A group of older studies draw on church court and other legal records, including Susan Dwyer Amussen, *An Ordered Society: Gender and Class in Early Modern England* (Oxford: Oxford University Press, 1988), Laura Gowing, *Domestic Dangers: Women, Words, and Sex in Early Modern London* (Oxford: Oxford University Press, 1996), and Alexandra Shepard, *Meanings of Manhood in Early Modern England* (Oxford: Oxford University Press, 2003). The context of marital violence is thoughtfully outlined in Susan Dwyer Amussen, '"Being Stirred to Much Unquietness": Violence and Domestic Violence in Early Modern England', *Journal of Women's History* 6/2 (1994), and Jessica Malay's *The Case of Mistress Mary Hampson* (Stanford, CA: Stanford University Press, 2014) presents a startling, detailed case study.

On space and objects, good starting points are Amanda Flather, *Gender and Space in Early Modern England* (Woodbridge: Boydell Press, 2007), Laura Gowing,'"The Freedom of the Streets": Women and Social Space, 1560–1640' in Mark S. R. Jenner and Paul Griffiths (eds), *Londinopolis: Essays in the Cultural and Social History of Early Modern London* (Manchester: Manchester University Press, 2000), and Tara Hamling and Catherine Richardson (eds), *Everyday Objects: Medieval and Early Modern Material Culture and Its Meanings* (Aldershot: Ashgate, 2010).

The field of women's work has been transformed in the last decade, and is best approached first through the articles by Alexandra Shepard, 'Crediting Women in the Early Modern English Economy', *History Workshop Journal* 78 (2015), Jane Whittle and Mark Hailwood, 'The Gender Division of Labour in Early Modern England', *Economic History Review* 73/1 (2020), Jane Whittle, 'A Critique of Approaches to "Domestic Work": Women, Work and the Pre-Industrial Economy', *Past & Present* 243 (2019), and Amy Erickson, 'Married Women's Occupations in Eighteenth-Century London', *Continuity and Change* 23/2 (2008), all of which draw on the 'verb-oriented' approach that measures time spent rather than occupations named. Further work on the distinctive context of London includes Eleanor Hubbard, *City Women: Money, Sex, and the Social Order in Early Modern London* (Oxford: Oxford University Press, 2012), Tim Reinke-Williams, *Women, Work and Sociability in Early Modern London* (Basingstoke: Palgrave Macmillan, 2014), and Laura Gowing, *Ingenious Trade: Women and Work in Seventeenth-Century London* (Cambridge: Cambridge University Press, 2021). On women in guilds, see Sarah Birt, 'Women, Guilds and the Tailoring Trades: The Occupational Training of Merchant Taylors' Company Apprentices in Early Modern London', *London Journal* 46/2 (2021) and Laura Gowing, 'Girls on Forms: Apprenticing Young Women in Seventeenth-Century London' *Journal of British Studies* 55/3 (2016). Service and apprenticeship are discussed, respectively, in Charmian Mansell, 'Beyond the

Home: Space and Agency in the Experiences of Female Service in Early Modern England', *Gender & History* 33/1 (2021) and Ilana Krausman Ben-Amos, 'Women Apprentices in the Trade and Crafts of Early Modern Bristol', *Continuity and Change* 6/2 (1991). Paula Humfrey's *The Experience of Domestic Service for Women in Early Modern London* (London: Routledge, 2016) usefully includes court depositions.

The fullest treatment of women and property, and legal issues around inheritance, is Amy Erickson's *Women and Property in Early Modern England* (London: Routledge, 1993). Subsequent work has laid out women's involvement in lending and investment: Craig Muldrew, '"A Mutual Assent of Her Mind"? Women, Debt, Litigation and Contract in Early Modern England', *History Workshop Journal* 55 (2003), Judith Spicksley, 'Usury Legislation, Cash and Credit: the Development of the Female Investor in the Late Tudor and Stuart Periods', *Economic History Review* 61/2 (2008), Amy M. Froide, *Silent Partners: Women as Public Investors during Britain's Financial Revolution, 1690–1750* (Oxford: Oxford University Press, 2016), and (in women's landownership) Amanda Capern et al., *Women and the Land, 1500–1900* (Woodbridge: Boydell, 2019). An innovative and stimulating comparative perspective is provided in Maria Ågren and Amy Erickson (eds), *The Marital Economy in Scandinavia and Britain, 1400–1900* (Aldershot: Ashgate, 2005), and Erickson's article, 'Coverture and Capitalism' in *History Workshop Journal* 59 (2005) argues for a relationship between the restrictions of property law and the development of financial markets.

Single women's economic lives provide an important contrast to the restrictions on married women: independence, enterprise and usefulness as well as constraints are examined in Amy Froide, *Never Married: Singlewomen in Early Modern England* (Oxford: Oxford University Press, 2005), Pamela Sharpe, 'Dealing With Love: The Ambiguous Independence of the Single Woman in Early Modern England', *Gender & History* 11/2 (1999), and Judith Spicksley, '"Fly with a Duck in Thy Mouth": Single Women as Sources of Credit in Seventeenth-Century England', *Social History* 32 (2007).

On the gender dynamics of community order, a classic piece by Keith Wrightson, 'The Politics of the Parish in Early Modern England', in Adam Fox et al. (eds), *The Experience of Authority in Early Modern England* (Basingstoke: Palgrave, 1996) works well with Bernard Capp's stress on neighbourly relations in *When Gossips Meet: Women, Family and Neighbourhood in Early Modern England* (Oxford: Oxford University Press, 2003). Richelle Munkhoff, 'Searchers of the Dead: Authority, Marginality, and the Interpretation of Plague in England, 1574–1665', *Gender & History* 11/1 (1999), examines an important parish role of women. Social histories of the 1980s explored the ritual regulations of community life, led by David Underdown, 'The Taming of the Scold: The Enforcement of Patriarchal Authority in Early Modern England', in Anthony Fletcher and John Stevenson (eds), *Order and Disorder in Early Modern England* (Cambridge: Cambridge University Press, 1985), and Martin Ingram, 'Ridings, Rough Music, and Mocking Rhymes in Early Modern

England', in Barry Reay (ed.), *Popular Culture in Seventeenth-Century England* (London: Routledge, 1985). A subsequent wave of work on legal records highlighted insult, credit and reputation: see among others Laura Gowing, 'Gender and the Language of Insult in Early Modern London'. *History Workshop Journal* 35 (1993), Steve Hindle, 'The Shaming of Margaret Knowsley: Gossip, Gender and the Experience of Authority in Early Modern England', *Continuity and Change* 9/3 (1994), and Bernard Capp, 'The Double Standard Revisited: Plebeian Women and Male Sexual Reputation In Early Modern England', *Past & Present* 162 (1999).

On crime, law and gender, the essays and introduction by Alexandra Shepard and Tim Stretton in a special issue of *Journal of British Studies* 58/4 (2019) focus on 'Women Negotiating the Boundaries of Justice in Britain, 1300–1700'. Tim Stretton and K. J. Kesselring (eds), *Married Women and the Law: Coverture in England and the Common Law World* (Montreal: McGill-Queen's University Press, 2014) examines coverture in depth, and for a concise explanation of women's property and legal rights see Stretton, 'Women, Property and Law' in Anita Pacheco (ed.), *A Companion to Early Modern Women's Writing* (Oxford: Wiley, 2002). Jenny Kermode and Garthine Walker (eds), *Women, Crime and the Courts in Early Modern England* (London: Routledge, 1994), opened a new field, followed by specific works on crime and litigation, including Garthine Walker, *Crime, Gender and Social Order in Early Modern England* (Cambridge: Cambridge University Press, 2003), Laura Gowing, *Domestic Dangers: Women, Words and Sex in Early Modern London* (Oxford: Oxford University Press, 1996), and Tim Stretton, *Women Waging Law in Elizabethan England* (Cambridge: Cambridge University Press, 1998). Useful starting points on gender and English witchcraft include Diane Purkiss, 'Women's Stories of Witchcraft in Early Modern England: The House, the Body, the Child', *Gender & History* 7/3 (1995), and Malcolm Gaskill, 'Masculinity and Witchcraft in Seventeenth-Century England' in Alison Rowlands (eds), *Witchcraft and Masculinities in Early Modern Europe* (Basingstoke: Palgrave, 2009).

The history of friendship includes much on masculinity, such as Alan Bray and Michel Rey, 'The Body of the Friend: Continuity and Change in Masculine Friendship in the Seventeenth Century', in Tim Hitchcock and Michele Cohen (eds), *English Masculinities, 1660–1800* (Harlow: Longman, 1999), and recently more on women's friendship: the shining example is Frances Harris, *Transformations of Love: The Friendship of John Evelyn and Margaret Godolphin* (Oxford: Oxford University Press, 2003), but see also Laura Gowing, Michael Hunter and Miri Rubin (eds), *Love, Friendship, and Faith in Europe, 1300–1800* (Basingstoke: Palgrave, 2005), and Amanda Herbert, *Female Alliances: Gender, Identity and Friendship in Early Modern Britain* (New Haven, CT: Yale University Press, 2014).

A valuable introduction to gender in the British Atlantic context is Susan Pearsall, 'Gender', in David Armitage and Michael J. Braddick (eds), *The British Atlantic World, 1500–1800* (Basingstoke: Macmillan, 2009). Two articles by Susan D. Amussen and Allyson M. Poska, 'Shifting the Frame: Trans-Imperial

Approaches to Gender in the Atlantic World', *Early Modern Women* 9/1 (2014) and 'Restoring Miranda: Gender and the Limits of European Patriarchy in the Early Modern Atlantic World', *Journal of Global History* 7/3 (2012), offer a more theoretical approach. On Caribbean slavery's impact on gender relations in Britain, see Amussen's *Caribbean Exchanges: Slavery and the Transformation of English Society, 1640–1700* (Durham, NC: University of North Carolina Press, 2007), and more generally on slavery, gender and capitalism, see Jennifer Morgan's *Reckoning with Slavery: Gender, Kinship, and Capitalism in the Early Black Atlantic* (Durham, NC: Duke University Press, 2021).

On women and politics, the essays in Hilda L. Smith (ed.), *Women Writers and the Early Modern British Political Tradition* (Cambridge: Cambridge University Press, 1998) are still central; see also Patricia Crawford's two articles, 'Public Duty, Conscience and Women in Early Modern England', in John Morrill et al. (eds), *Public Duty and Private Conscience in Seventeenth-Century England* (Oxford: Oxford University Press, 1992) and '"The Poorest She": Women and Citizenship in Early Modern England', in Michael Mendle (ed.), *The Putney Debates of 1647: The Army, the Levellers and the English State* (Cambridge: Cambridge University Press, 2001), which discusses voting and oaths. Gender in the Civil War has a rich historiography, led by Ann Hughes's essential *Gender and the English Revolution* (London: Routledge, 2011), and going back to Ellen McArthur's 'Women Petitioners and the Long Parliament', *The English Historical Review* 24/96 (1909). Marcus Nevitt, *Women and the Pamphlet Culture of Revolutionary England, 1640–1660* (Aldershot: Ashgate, 2006) explores the print world, and Jamie McDougall, 'Local Experiences of National Covenanting, 1638–43' in *The Scottish Historical Review* 99, Supplement 251 (December 2020), discusses women's covenanting. Phyllis Mack's definitive work on female Quakers, *Visionary Women: Ecstatic Prophecy in Seventeenth-Century England* (Berkeley, CA: University of California Press, 1995), reflects deeply on the operation of gender. Stuart political culture's reconfigurations of gender and power are examined in Rachel Weil, *Political Passions: Gender, the Family, and Political Argument in England, 1680–1714* (Manchester: Manchester University Press, 1999). On coffee houses and the public sphere, see Brian Cowan, 'What Was Masculine About the Public Sphere? Gender and the Coffeehouse Milieu in Post-Restoration England', *History Workshop Journal* 51 (2001).

All works on protest should have something to say on women's role; good starting points are John Walter, 'Faces in the Crowd: Gender and Age in the Early Modern English Crowd' in Berry and Foyster (eds), *The Family in Early Modern England*, Walter's article on Ann Carter, 'Grain Riots and Popular Attitudes to the Law: Maldon and the Crisis of 1629', in his *Crowds and Popular Politics in Early Modern England* (Manchester: Manchester University Press, 2006), and Andy Wood, *Riot, Rebellion and Popular Politics in Early Modern England* (Basingstoke: Palgrave, 2001). On sedition Sharon L. Jansen, *Dangerous Talk and Strange Behavior: Women and Popular Resistance to the Reforms of Henry VIII* (New York: Palgrave Macmillan, 1996) provides rich detail on four Tudor women, and ordinary women's speech is discussed in Andy Wood, 'The Queen is "a Goggyll Eyed Hoore": Gender and Seditious Speech in Early Modern England', in Nicholas Tyacke (ed.), *The English Revolution c.1590–1720: Politics, Religion and Communities* (Manchester: Manchester University Press, 2007). Custom and memory are also critical: see Nicola Whyte, 'Custodians of Memory: Women and Custom in Rural England c. 1550–1700', *Cultural and Social History* 8/2 (2011).

On monarchy, Cynthia Herrup's 'The King's Two Genders', *Journal of British Studies* 45/3 (2006), offers a cogent analysis of gender and royal power; on specific monarchs, their courts and their representations, see Carole Levin *'The Heart and Stomach of a King': Elizabeth I and the Politics of Sex and Power* (Philadelphia, PA: Pennsylvania State University Press, 1994), Anna Whitelock, *Elizabeth's Bedfellows: An Intimate History of the Queen's Court* (London: Bloomsbury, 2014), and Judith Richards, 'Mary Tudor as "Sole Quene"? Gendering Tudor Monarchy', *Historical Journal* 40 (1997).

# References

Amussen, Susan D. (2007) *Caribbean Exchanges: Slavery and the Transformation of English Society, 1640–1700*. Durham, NC: University of North Carolina Press.

Amussen, Susan D. (2021) 'Gender, Inversion and the Causes of the Civil War'. In Paul Halliday, Eleanor Hubbard and Scott Sowerby (eds), *Revolutionising Politics: Culture and Conflict in England, 1620–1660*. Manchester: Manchester University Press.

Bendall, Sarah Anne (2014) 'To Write a Distick upon It: Busks and the Language of Courtship and Sexual Desire in Sixteenth- and Seventeenth-Century England'. *Gender & History* 26/2, 199–222.

Bennett, Judith M. (1996) *Ale, Beer and Brewsters in England: Women's Work in a Changing World, 1300–1600*. Oxford: Oxford University Press.

Bennett, Judith M. (2006) *History Matters: Patriarchy and the Challenge of Feminism*. Philadelphia, PA: University of Pennsylvania Press.

Bray, Alan and Michel Rey (1999) 'The Body of the Friend: Continuity and Change in the Seventeenth Century'. In Tim Hitchcock and Michèle Cohen (eds), *English Masculinities 1660–1800*. London: Longman.

Breitenberg, Mark (1996) *Anxious Masculinity in Early Modern England*. Cambridge: Cambridge University Press.

Brown, Kathleen (1996) *Good Wives, Nasty Wenches and Anxious Patriarchs: Gender, Race and Power in Colonial Virginia*. Chapel Hill, NC: University of North Carolina Press.

Capp, Bernard (2014) '"Jesus Wept" But Did the Englishman? Masculinity and Emotion in Early Modern England'. *Past & Present* 224: 75–108.

Clark, Alice (1992) *Working Life of Women in the Seventeenth Century*. Edited by Amy L. Erickson. London: Routledge.

Connell, Raewyn (2009) *Gender*. Cambridge: Polity.

Crawford, Patricia (2001) '"The Poorest She": Women and Citizenship in Early Modern England'. In Michael Mendle (ed.), *The Putney Debates of 1647: The Army, the Levellers and the English State*. Cambridge: Cambridge University Press.

De Moor, Tine and Jan Luiten Van Zanden (2010) 'Girl Power: The European Marriage Pattern and Labour Markets in the North Sea Region in the Late Medieval and Early Modern Period'. *Economic History Review* 63/1: 1–33.

De Vries, Jan (1994) 'The Industrial Revolution and the Industrious Revolution'. *The Journal of Economic History* 54/2: 249–270.

Erickson, Amy L. (1992) 'Introduction'. In Alice Clark, *Working Life of Women in the Seventeenth Century*. London: Routledge.

Erickson, Amy L. (2005) 'Coverture and Capitalism'. *History Workshop Journal* 59: 1–16.

Erickson, Amy L. (2008) 'Married Women's Occupations in Eighteenth-Century London'. *Continuity and Change* 23/2: 267–307.

Ewen, Misha (2021) 'The Life of Edward Francis: Black History at the Tower of London'. Retrieved from https://blog.hrp.org.uk/curators/the-life-of-edward-francis-black-history-at-the-tower-of-london. Accessed 18 November 2021.

Fisher, Will (2001) 'The Renaissance Beard: Masculinity in Early Modern England'. *Renaissance Quarterly* 54/1: 155–187.

Fissell, Mary E. (2004) 'The Politics of Reproduction in the English Reformation'. *Representations* 87/1: 43–81.

Froide, Amy M. (2005) *Never Married: Singlewomen in Early Modern England*. Oxford: Oxford University Press.

Froide, Amy M. (2016) *Silent Partners: Women as Public Investors during Britain's Financial Revolution, 1690–1750*. Oxford: Oxford University Press.

Gouge, William (1622). *Of Domesticall Duties: Eight Treatises*. London.

Gray, Catharine (2001). 'Feeding on the Seed of the Woman: Dorothy Leigh and the Figure of Maternal Dissent'. *ELH* 68/3: 563–592.

Griffiths, Paul (1998) 'Meanings of Nightwalking in Early Modern England'. *Seventeenth Century* 13/2: 212–238.

Hall, Kim (1996) 'Culinary Spaces, Colonial Spaces: The Gendering of Sugar in the Seventeenth Century'. In Valerie Traub, M. Lindsay Kaplan and Dympna Callaghan (eds), *Feminist Readings of Early Modern Culture: Emerging Subjects*. Cambridge: Cambridge University Press.

Harris, Frances (2003) *Transformations of Love: The Friendship of Margaret Evelyn and John Godolphin*. Oxford: Oxford University Press.

Herrup, Cynthia (2006) 'The King's Two Genders'. *Journal of British Studies* 45/3: 493–510.

Hughes, Ann (2011) *Gender and the English Revolution*. London: Routledge.

Hunt, Margaret (2004) 'Women and the Fiscal- Imperial State in the Late Seventeenth and Early Eighteenth Centuries'. In Kathleen Wilson (ed), *A New Imperial History: Culture, Identity and Modernity in Britain and the Empire, 1660–1840*. Cambridge: Cambridge University Press.

Kaufmann, Miranda (2017) *Black Tudors: The Untold Story*. London: OneWorld.

Kent, E. J. (2005) 'Masculinity and Male Witches in Old and New England, 1593–1680'. *History Workshop Journal* 60: 69–92.

Laqueur, Thomas (1990) *Making Sex: Body and Gender From the Greeks To Freud*. Cambridge, MA: Harvard University Press.

Mendelson, Sara Heller and Patricia Crawford (1995) 'Sexual Identities in Early Modern England: The Marriage of Two Women in 1680'. *Gender & History* 7/3: 362–377.

Miller, Jonah (2019) 'The Touch of the State: Stop and Search in England, c.1660–1750'. *History Workshop Journal* 87: 52–71.

Morgan, Jennifer L. (1997) '"Some Could Suckle over Their Shoulder": Male Travelers, Female Bodies, and the Gendering of Racial Ideology, 1500–1770'. *The William and Mary Quarterly* 54/1: 167–192.

Morgan, Jennifer L. (2004) *Laboring Women: Reproduction and Gender in New World Slavery*. Philadelphia, PA: University of Pennsylvania Press.

Newman, Simon (2022) *Freedom Seekers: Escaping from Slavery in Restoration London*. London: University of London Press.

Pateman, Carole (1988) *The Sexual Contract*. Stanford, CA: Stanford University Press.

Peters, Christine (2003) *Patterns of Piety: Women, Gender and Religion in Late Medieval and Reformation England*. Cambridge: Cambridge University Press.

Purkiss, Diane (1995) 'Women's Stories of Witchcraft in Early Modern England: The House, the Body, the Child'. *Gender & History* 7/3: 408–432.

Sharpe, Pamela (1999) 'Dealing with Love: The Ambiguous Independence of the Single Woman in Early Modern England'. *Gender & History* 11/3: 209–232.

Shepard, Alexandra (2005) 'From Anxious Patriarchs to Refined Gentlemen? Manhood in Britain, circa 1500–1700'. *Journal of British Studies* 44/2: 281–295.

Shepard, Alexandra (2015) 'Crediting Women in the Early Modern English Economy'. *History Workshop Journal* 78: 1–24.

Shepard, Alexandra (2017) 'Pleasures and Pains of Breastfeeding in England *c*.1600–*c*.1800'. In M. J. Braddick, Joanna Innes and Paul Slack (eds), *Suffering and Happiness in England 1550-1850: Narratives and Representations*. Oxford: Oxford University Press.

Shoemaker, Robert B. (1999) 'Reforming Male Manners: Public Insult and the Decline of Violence in London, 1660–1740'. In Tim Hitchcock (ed.), *English Masculinities, 1660–1800*. London: Longman.

Spicksley, Judith (ed.). (2012) *The Business and Household Accounts of Joyce Jeffreys, Spinster of Hereford*. Oxford: Oxford University Press.

Traub, Valerie (2002) *The Renaissance of Lesbianism in Early Modern England*. Cambridge: Cambridge University Press.

Underdown, David (1985) 'The Taming of the Scold: The Enforcement of Patriarchal Authority in Early Modern England'. In Anthony Fletcher and John Stevenson (eds), *Order and Disorder in Early Modern England*. Cambridge: Cambridge University Press.

Weil, Rachel (1999) *Political Passions: Gender, the Family, and Political Argument in England, 1680–1714*. Manchester: Manchester University Press.

Weil, Rachel (2013) 'Politics and Gender in Crisis in David Underdown's "The Taming of the Scold"'. *History Compass* 11/3: 381–388.

Wiesner-Hanks, Merry E. (2008) 'Do Women Need the Renaissance?'. *Gender & History* 20/3: 539–557.

Wrightson, Keith (1980) 'Two Concepts of Order: Justices, Constables and Jurymen in Seventeenth-Century England'. In John Brewer and John Styles (eds), *An Ungovernable People: The English and their Law in the Seventeenth and Eighteenth Centuries*. London: Hutchinson.

Wrigley, Edward A. and Roger Schofield (1981) *The Population History of England, 1541–1871: A Reconstruction*. Cambridge: Cambridge University Press.

# Index

Entries in *italics* refer to illustrations.